ISTRIA

HISTORY · CULTURE · ART HERITAGE

ANTUN TRAVIRKA

FORUM

Fields under Učka

Geographically speaking Istria can be defined as a peninsula whose northern border is the line stretching from Miljski bay (Muggia) in the immediate vicinity of Trieste to the northernmost point of Prelučki bay to the northwest of Rijeka. The southermost point, the tip of the peninsula, is the cape of Kamenjak located southeast of Pola. Although the Istrian peninsula, with its triangular shape and its dimensions (circa 1.200 square miles), is without doubt the largest and the most significant land mass of the broken Adriatic coast it can be explained both regarding its geographical structure and its historical definition of space as a piece of land between two deep and important seawater bays - the Trieste bay to the northwest and the Kvarner bay to the east. Political influences and the gravitational pull of political, economic and cultural forces on the Istrian peninsula converged, down through the centuries, around these two areas so that the interpretation of historical processes and culture is much more complex than its simple geographical rendering. Even the very structure of the morphologically various geographical wholes on the terrain of

Left:
View from the air of the wider country around Poreč

Istria contributes to the complexity of explaining Istria as a unique geographical concept.

Istria is separated from the hinterland by limestone mountain ranges and the craggy heights of Triestian Kras and Ćićarije mountains. The space of the peninsula itself can be divided into three geomorphologically wholly different regions.

The hilly northern and northeastern edge of the peninsula, owing to its meagre vegetation and the bare and bright surface of the Karst valley, is called White Istria. White Istria receives the largest amount of rainwater but the water disappears underground so that arable land is reduced to the lowlands of the Karst valley. This poor region is sparsely inhabited and the people there have traditionally been occupied with raising small flocks of livestock. A part of White Istria consisting of the Učka mountain steeply descends into the sea. The littoral population of the eastern coast of the Istrian peninsula has always been turned to the sea and shipping occupations. In recent times it has taken up tourism.

To the southwest of White Istria lies a space which is morphologically much richer. This is a hilly region crisscrossed by rivers and valleys, rich in water and vegetation. The soil is not exceptionally rich but nevertheless grains, fruits, vineyards as well as bovine cattle were to be found

5

The river Mirņa near where it flows into Tarski bay

here throughout the centuries. As this space is characterised by deciduous vegetation, gray colours dominate throughout the winter and this is where its name Gray Istria comes from. Since prehistoric times settlements were raised here on the slopes and hills which overlooked the river valleys and the fields. Antique towns and Medieval fortified settlements as well as many villages having their own defence walls arose on the foundations of numerous prehistoric hill-forts, castles. Some of the significant city centers such as Kopar, which through centuries was the administrative center of Venetian Istria, and Pirana, whose famous salt works through ages supplied the Venetian republic with this strategically important resource, arose in the north of Gray Istria. Oil findings were abundant in Gray Istria so that in its southeastern part and especially in the region of Raša and Labin mining has had a long tradition.

Islands in front of Rovinj. Below St John on the Sea, in the middle Sturag and St Andrew (Red island)

The southern and western coast of Istria are characterised by a wide belt of plateau land which gently slopes towards the sea. The coast is very uneven with many coves, deep bays and rivermouths. Within the string of islets encompassing the coast one has to set apart the Brioni islands stretching along the coast from Poreč to Rovinj. This whole region has preserved a covering of salient red topsoil from which derives the name Red Istria. This is a relatively densely populated region. Important urban centers such as Poreč, Rovinj and especially Pola, as well as a number of smaller

Istrian landscape

towns such as Umag, Novigrad and Vrsar rose along the coast of western Istria. Agricultural production is highly developed in Red Istria while important industries have developed in the urban zone of Pola. The entire coast of Red Istria is today a touristic region, one of the most important and most developed tourist zones in the Republic of Croatia.

Due to historical circumstances and the national dispersion of the population, its cultures, languages and traditions, nowadays the geographical region of the Istrian peninsula is divided amongst three neighbouring countries that maintain friendly relations.

Only a small part of Istria, the northern side of the Miljski peninsula which encloses the southern side of the port of Trieste, belongs to the Republic of Italy.

The Slovenian coastal region, with the Kopar bay and part of the Piran bay up to the Dragonja rivermouth as well as the greater part of Kras in the hinterland, is part of the Republic of Slovenia and provides it with its access to the sea.

The undoubtedly largest part of the territory covered by the geographical concept of Istria, namely the entire corpus of the Istria peninsula south of the Dragonja rivermouth up to the uppermost tip of Prelučki bay to the southeast, is a constituent and a very significant part of the Republic of Croatia. Croatian Istria encompasses a very significant part of White and the biggest part of Gray Istria and the entire space of Red Istria.

Istria is located on a very significant juncture of the European continent, at a place where two mountain chains almost join - the Alps and the Dinara highlands. The northern plateaus and the hilly portions of Istria are a part of the broader space of the so-called Adriatic doors, the passage between the above mentioned mountain chains. From the Furlanian lowlands to the west and the Postojna passage to the northeast they represent the main pathway through which numerous peoples and civilisations circulated in past ages. These movements included both the attempts to penetrate and conquer the European continent from the Italic peninsula and, in the opposite direction, the centuries long campaigns to infiltrate and conquer the stupendous wealth which had been built and collected by various civilisations in Italy. Such a turbulent space inevitably reflected many historical events which brought about frequent migrations and

Twilight on the Liburnian coastline

exoduses and, accordingly, changes in the makeup of the population, its tradition and culture. Millenial political contentions, incessant tensions and the division of this small space amongst different countries as well as the broader strategic influence of domineering European powers fatefully influenced the specific quality of life and the variety of cultural influences within this region.

Simply stated, Istria is a unique place on which three dominant European ethnic groups have come into contact on a small space down through the centuries; the Romans, the Germans and the Slavs. Their political relationships have conditioned the political divisions on Istrian soil up to our own days.

Archeological findings attest to the fact that the Istrian peninsula had been settled by man as early as the Old Stone Age. Many remains of prehistoric buildings can be found from the Bronze Age (the second millenium BC) on the hills and high grounds, as well as remains of temples whose shape and stone building material remind us of "kažun" - the traditional stone-wall dwellings of Istrian shepherds. During the Iron Age (first millennium BC) Istria was relatively densely populated, in large part by Illyrian tribes. The Histri, an Illyrian tribe who gave the peninsula its name, settled the region of western and central Istria, from the river Timavus (Timavo, Reka) up all the way to the slopes of Učka. The region from the river Raša eastward including the Kvarner coast was settled by another Illyrian tribe, the Liburnians. Their territory stretched across today's Croatian seaboard up to the river Krka in Dalmatia. The northern peripheral parts of Istria on Kras were inhabited by the Japods, a tribe of Illyrian-Celtic ancestry. The Histri were generally shepherds and farmers whereas the Liburnians were excellent seamen, merchants but also pirates. The remains of Illyrian material culture are in evidence throughout Istria, especially the ruins of fort-hill settlements (castles) on high grounds and hills whose walls had been built with drystone technique using large stone blocs. Quite a number of these were real, organised cities which bears witness to the high level of civilisation amongst the Illyrians. As has been already said, these castles provided the foundations on which most of the Istrian urban settlements were afterwards built. The Illyrian tribes in Istria had contacts with Greek civilisation which is

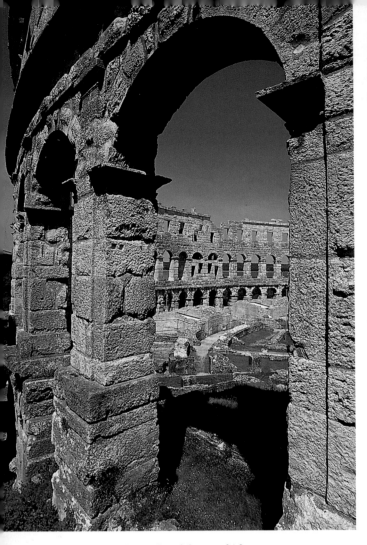

Pola, through the vaults of the amphitheatre

Pola, view of the eastern side of the Sergievan triumphal arch

corroborated by the myth of the Argonauts and the legend of the conquest of Pola.

When, during their campaigns of expansion, the Romans conquered the land of the Veneta people they erected in 181 BC the powerful fortification Akvilea on the river Tagliamento which was to serve not only as a defence of the eastern borders but also as a base for continuing the movement eastward. The Romans waged a war against the Illyrians of Istria in 178 and 177 BC. A long period of Roman domination commenced with the defeat of the Histri under the walls of their main city Nesactium in 177. Occupying the greater part of Istria the Romans implemented an expedient and efficient process of colonialisation. In spite of powerful resistance mounted by the Histri and their uprising in 129 BC, the Roman conquerers wholly subjugated the Illyrian indigenous population.

The greater part of the population was forced to flee and more than 15.000 colonialists were brought from the Italic peninsula. The Romans established the colonies of Pola, Poreč (Parentium), Trieste (Tergeste) and Labin (Albona). A large portion of the land was divided among the veteran soldiers while large homesteads were established on the most fertile land. Latifundias with luxury country villas were erected there. Being expert builders the Romans constructed a very good road, Via Flavia, which led from Pola to Aquileia from where the Roman regent ruled the Istrian possessions. The Roman conquest continued to

On the next page:
Pola, the facade of the temple of Augustus,
beginning of the Ist century

Poreč, fragment of a floor mosaic from the IVth century with a symbolical depiction of fish.
It was found on the site of the earliest constructed Christian oratorium north of the Euphrasian basilica.

the east so that in the year 50 BC the Liburnians were subjugated and with them the eastern, Liburnian part of Istria. The great reforms in the organisation of the state which were implemented by the first Roman emperor Octavius Augustus at the change of the millennium included the modification of the border so that the border of Italy was moved from the river Rižana in the bay of Kopar to the river Raša. By this action the greater part of the territory of Istria became a part of the Italic region. Eastern, Liburnian Istria was joined to the province of Dalmatia. Romanized and pacified, for more than six centuries Istria remained within the framework of the Roman empire till the fall of its western part in 476 AD. The large migrations of peoples which during late Antiquity changed the makeup of the world of the time were reflected on the Istrian peninsula more as processions of displaced persons than as arenas of warfare. Large movements and decisive battles were taking place somewhat to the north and the west. The slave system was being demolished and a new one, based on serfdom, came into being and was to remain in force throughout these regions almost up to our own days.

After the breakup of the Western Roman empire Istria came under the jurisdiction of Odoakar. After his defeat, from the year 489 AD it was a part of Teodoric's state of the Eastern Goths. During the first part of the VIth century the Byzantium emperor Justian waged a long, twelve year war against the Ostrogothic state with the intention of renewing the Western Roman empire. Already by 539 AD Istria was, as a part of Byzantium, joined to the Ravena exarchate. Byzantium rule will remain in Istria until 788 AD. This was a period of the renewal of life and the construction of many important architectural works. Amongst the most important examples one ought to mention the architectural complex in the Euphrasian basilica in Poreč and the great basilica of St Mary Formose in Pola.

During the VIth and VIIth century there were more and more raids waged by the Slavs and the Avars onto the Istrian peninsula. In 600 AD Pope Gregory the first complained to the bishop of Salona that he was greatly grieved because of the Slavs making inroads into Italy across Istria. Originally these invaders appeared under the generic name of Slavs whereas the tribal differentiation into Croats and Slovenes

Poreč, the Euphrasian basilica, the facade with remains of mosaic and the nartex

took place quite later. Since the troubled times brought about the decimation of the Roman and the Romanized inhabitants, the need for agricultural labourers turned the Slavs into the new settlers.

An especially widespread settlement of Istria by the Slavs occured after 788 AD when the Istrian lands came under the dominion of Charlemagne's Frankish state. Establishing a highly developed system of feudal relationships the Frankish state brought in a large number of Slavs who as serfs cultivated the land of the dispossessed Istrian Roman landowners, especially the holdings of the citizens of the Istrian cities. The conflict between the old and new order was evinced by the Rižana assembly in 804 AD which Charlemagne convened and sent his emissaries to give a hearing to the complaints voiced by the cities of western Istria and by the bishop of Trieste. The demand for the return of the older privileges of the cities was only partially heeded by returning self-government but without the return of the usurped land holdings. The process of introducing the new feudal system was soon resumed with full intensity. Frankish connections and their patronage of the newly established Croatian state in the areas of Dalmatia and the Croatian littoral were the causes for the growing role of Croatian people in the Istrian hinterland. According to the account of the Byzantium emperor Constantin Porfirogenet the Croatian state in the Xth century had spread all the way to the river Raša and included the region of Labinština, Učka and Snježnik. In this manner the Croats penetrated over Plomin and Labin towards Pola and over Pićan into the inner regions of the peninsula. By the XIth century the surrounding hinterland of all the coastal cities was inhabited by a Croatian population so that many roads were known as Slav roads (via sclavonica). The Croats in Istria organized themselves into broader community districts with perfects at their head. The oldest written information concerning the district organisation of the Istrian Croats dates from a XIIth century document which in 1199 mentioned the perfect Dražic from Gračišće.

Frankish feudal rule was characterised by the detachment of individual regions, duchies, and putting them under the rule of different Frankish vassals. Thusly Istria together with Furlania initially constituted the Aquileian mark, subordinated to the Bavarian dukedom. According to the division of the Frankish state in 843 the oldest grandson of Charlemagne, emperor Lotar, received control over Istria as a constituent part of Italy as a whole. A number of changes of feudal lords was to follow after which Istria was separated from Bavaria and joined to the dukedom of Carantania (Koruška). By the middle of the XIth century Istria had become a separate duchy which was gifted by the German emperors as inheritable feudal land to different aristocratic families. Some of the rulers over this territory began to detach individual fiefs. In the middle of the XIth century the duke Ulrich Orlamunde separated the so-called Merania region, making up the eastern Istrian coastline from Raša to Rijeka. This piece of land remained separated for more than 150 years. Another separate unit was the Pazin duchy which was given by the Poreč bishops as a fief to the dukes of Gorica. In 1209 the Aquileian patriarch Volger received from the German emperors the Istrian dukedom as a fief of the Aquileian church. Istria retained this status up to 1420. The Pazin duchy remained a separate territory. Throughout the period of domination by the Aquileian patriarchs the Istrian coastal cities with their powerful tradition of free municipalities and with their predominantly Roman population put up a strong resistance to continental rule. In this they sought support from their ever more powerful ally - the Republic of Venice. The process by which the Venetians

13

Ruins of Dvigrad

gradually gained more and more influence and spread their rule over the Istrian peninsula lasted more than four centuries. Behaving in most instances as an ally and the protector of the coastal cities, although sometimes engaging with them in acts of hostilities, the Venetians gradually exerted their influence and afterwards their control over the cities and the coast of western Istria. When the power of the Aquileian patriarch had disappeared in the middle of the XVth century Istria was put under full control by Venice excepting the Pazin duchy and the Kvarner littoral. In the meantime, at the end of the XIVth century the Pazin duchy had been inherited by the Hapsburgs who also came into possession of the eastern coast of Istria. In such a manner, all of Istria was divided between the Austrian-German and the Venetain-Romanic governmental, political and civilisational sphere.

Saint Lovreč Pazenatički, Ramanesque-Gothic tower-belfry. To the right, the apses of the parish church of St Martin

The administrative center of Istria under Venice was Kopar but there was no such thing as an integral government. The manager ("Captain") of the rural part of the Venetian domain ("paisanatico") had his center in Saint Lovreč Pazenatički, while the Venetian military commander of the region which bordered the Austrian lands had his seat first in the military fortification of Rašpor and afterwards in Buzet.

Throughout the period Pazin remained the center of the Hapsburg possession in Istria. As the Hapsburgs did not maintain such a tight influence over their lands the position of the Croatian populace under their rule was a bit more favourable. It was on the territory of the Pazin duchy that numerous examples of Croatian literacy written with the characteristic Glagolitic script came into being. The oldest writings date back to the XIth century. From Istria come the

documents. This was also the first time that the language spoken by the people in Istria was explicitly refered to as the "Croatian language".

At the end of the XIVth century, and especially during the XVth century, many Istrian churches, particularly those in the Pazin duchy, were painted with Gothic frescos which evinced specific characteristics in that the folk figurative tradition intertwined with features of the international Gothic style. For the most part these were works made by native masters or those from the neighbouring regions. Owing to their freshness and immediacy they represent an important and a distinct body of Late Medieval art works on the territory of Croatia.

During the XVth century, many new public buildings and private palaces in the style of the decorative Venetian florid Gothic were constructed on the territory under Venetian administration, but particularly in the coastal cities. This endowed the urban texture of the Istrian cities with a new characteristic appearance.

Beram, detail of fresco with scene of the Dance of Death (1474)

Poreč, Gothic triforium from a palace in Decuman street

many Glagolitic missals and other church books that are today kept in different European libraries. The translations of popular works of Medieval Europaen literature were written in the Glagolitic script. Many manuscripts and documents have been preserved. The most significant Croatian Glagolitic text is "Istarski razvod" (The Istrian Divide), a Croatian Medieval legal document which precisely allocates the division of the Istrian districts, communes and fiefs between the Aquileian patriarch, the Pazin dukes and Venice. The text had been written during a longer period of time, from the last third of the XIIIth to the end of the XIVth century, and is an exceptionally important legal, historical and cultural document which bears witness to the Istrian conditions of the time and to the fact that the Croats in Istria had very early put common law into written

Extensive outbreaks of the plague occured in the XVIth century on the territory of Istria and they decimated the population leaving whole regions desolate and empty. During the same century the region saw a large movement of people who were fleeing the oncoming Turks and their conquest of southeastern Europe. The waves of migration mostly came through the Hapsburgian part of Istria but the newcomers also settled throughout the abandoned Venetian territory. The new inhabitants of Istria were mostly Croats but there were also Montenegrins, Albanians, Rumanians, Vlachs and Greeks. In Venetian Istria, especially in Puljština, settlers from the vicinity of Padova and from Furlania had also arrived but because of difficult conditions this act of colonialization did not succeed. The second part of the XVIth century was also marked by the reformation movement in the church which had amongst the learned people of Istria its protagonists. Matija Vlačić Illyric (1520-1575), an Istrian man from Labin, became one of the pillars of the Protestant movement in Germany.

In 1615 the tensions that had periodically been breaking out between the Venetian and the Austrian part of Istria turned into an open war which devastated Istria. By the end of the XVIIth century the Turkish menace was waning in this part of Europe and as a consequence the migrations slackened. At this time and especially during the XVIIIth century the renovation of many sacral buildings got under way in the Baroque style. Numerous palaces, country castles and utilitarian buildings throughout Istria were done in the same Baroque style.

The Venetian republic was abolished by Napoleon's conquest of Italy and the peace treaty in Campoformia in 1797. Its possessions, including Istria, were given to Austria. The Austrian administration was short-lived because already in 1805 Istria fell under Franch management and was annexed to the Kingdom of Italy. According to the Wien peace treaty in 1808 Hapsburgian Istria was taken away from Austria and connected to the other part which was separated from the Kingdom of Italy. In such a manner the entire territo-

Scene from old Labin

ry of Istria was connected to the new Napoleonic state organisation - the Illyrian provinces. This state unit was of short duration. After Napoleon's defeat in the "Battle of the Nations" near Leipzig in November 1813 Austria occupied Istria the next year and formed a province with Trieste as its capital. From 1825 Istria continued to be a single territorial whole but with its capital now in Pazin.

Owing to the great constitutional reforms of the Austrian empire during 1860 and 1861 Istria, bearing the name of a great duchy, became an Austrain province with a certain amount of decentralised administrative capabilities and its regional assembly in Poreč. From 1867 the perfect for Istria held his seat in Trieste.

From 1856 the Austrian empire built its main navy arsenal in Pola and from 1866 the city became the main harbour of the Austrian imperial navy. This contributed to its rapid urban development. In less than fifty years the population of Pola increased thirty times.

Poreč, the Istrian parliament hall was created after alternations made to the onetime Franciscan church.
The ceiling stucco-works for the onetime church were done by Guiseppe Monteventini in 1751

The entire second part of the XIXth century, including the years leading to WWI, was characterised in Istria by the struggle of the Croatian majority for national and political emancipation from the domination by the Italian minority. These tensions came in handy to the Austrian administration because they hid problems and muddled the real issue of German domination. The Croatian population was largely rural and, with the exception of the clergy of Croatian descent, badly educated. The Istrian city population was largely Italian. It was made up of large landowners, intellectuals, free professions, merchants, manufacturers and craftsmen. The goverment office workers had in large part come from north Italy. Because of election rules the relations in the Istrian assembly were favourable to the Italian minority.

The leader of the struggle of the Croats in Istria for emancipation was bishop Juraj Dobrila. He gave sober advise to the ruling circles about the need of cooperation between both nationalities of the Istrian population for their common good. Some years later, a prominent role in political activities aimed at the service of Croatian interests

was played by the well known Istrian lawyer and politician Matko Laginja.

The fall of the Austro-Hungarian monarchy in WWI signaled the end of Austrian rule over Istria. In accordance with the London agreement and in agreement with the Allied forces the Kingdom of Italy occupied the entire territory of Istria; according to the terms of the Rapallo treaty in 1920 the Kingdom of Yugoslavia was forced to surrender Istria to Italy.

When the Fascist movement took power in Italy it made attempts to Italianise Istria terrorising in unprecedental fashion the Croatian part of the population. All the Croatian schools, cultural institutions and associations were abolished. Croatian names were made over into Italian. It was prohibited to speak Croatian even within the confines of one's home. The consequence of these measures was a huge Croatian exodus into the Kingdom of Yugoslavia. It ought to be said that the policy of the Fascist government harassed the majority of the autochthonous Italian population as well, settling the abandoned areas with immigrants from backward Italian locations.

Rovinj, view from the island of St Catherine

In WWII Fascist Italy capitulated in September 1943 and Istria was occupied by German troops. The resistance movement in Istria was numerous and consisted of people from both communities. The fierce battles with the Germans took many lives and left behind destruction and desolation. During the German occupation Allied planes heavily bombed the Istrian cities Pola, Pazin and Poreč.

Twilight in Umag

On the basis of the so-called Pazin decisions from September 1943 and the decisions of the Territorial Anti-Fascist Council for the People's Liberation of Croatia from the same year, Istria, together with Rijeka, Zadar, the islands of Cres, Lošinj and Lastovo was rejoined, after the liberation in 1945 and the peace treaty with Italy signed in 1947, to its Croatian homeland which was then within the framework of Yugoslavia.

During this turbulent period full of ferment and in a state of flux the unnecessary and, above all, sad exodus of a part of the autochthonous Italian populace took place which brought about new changes in the demographic makeup of Istria.

The beginning of the 1990s saw the breakup of Yugoslavia and the borders between the formerly con-stituent federal republics of Croatia and Slovenia became the state borders between two sovereign countries.

Within independent and free Croatia Istria is an exceptionally important region. The importance of this western-most Croatian province does not only lie in its exceptional agricultural, industrial and particularly touristic potential and its enormous richness of monuments and artworks. Its position between three civilisations, its great historical experience of striving, suffering but also of coexistence has made the contemporary inhabitants of Istria wise, tolerant and open to the world. In its own specific fashion Istria belongs to those spaces where a new, future Europe is about to emerge.

Owing to its geographical structure, the course of its rivers, its plateaus, mountain ranges and its urban gravitational centers the space of Croatian Istria is divided into a number of smaller entities. The following description of individual localities and urban centers follows this division in the direction from the northwest towards the southeast part of the peninsula.

Left:
Pola, the Arena during large summer
musical and scenic manifestations

The historical center of Umag

Savudrija

Savudrija is the westernmost settlement on the Croatian Adriatic coast. It is located on a cape bearing the same name which closes off the southern side of the Piran bay. In the geographical perspective the cape of Savudrija is the westernmost point of the Balkan peninsula. The settlement has been built on a rocky coast covered with thickly growing pine and cypress. Because of the abundance of greenery and a series of small picturesque inlets Savudrija is an attractive touristic attraction. The cape is dominated by an old stone lighthouse whose height is 36 meters which was built under the Austrian administration back in 1826 at the time when other large Adriatic lighthouses were built. They were supposed to signalize the main navigable course from Trieste to Boka Kotorska. Nearby the lighthouse is the parish church of St John the Evangelist built in the XIXth century on the foundations of a much older Romanesque small church from the XIth century. In the vicinity of the nearby village Val Fonatan is the Romanesque church of St Lawrence built around 1200 AD.

According to legend the famous sea battle in which Venetian ships defeated the fleet of the German emperor Friedrich Barbarossa and Pope Alexander the IIIrd took place near Savudrija. In the XVIth century Domenico Tintorretto painted the scene of this famous sea battle for the doge's palace in Venice.

To the south of Savudrija is the archeological site of the Roman settlement Sipar which had existed in prehistoric times. The remains of the tower, a multi-naved storage place and a number of smaller rooms have been preserved from the earliest period. The settlement was destroyed during a devastating attack by pirates in 876 AD during the times of prince Domagoj.

Umag

A few kilometers south of the cape of Savudrija lies the very old and picturesque city of Umag. Built on a peninsula in the middle of a deeper horseshoe-shaped bay it was a well-protected anchorage from earliest times so that mention of the settlement Umacus is to be found in Roman

View from the air of Umag and the surrounding country. Piran bay in the background.

times. In the Middle Ages it was a possession of the Triestian bishops and later it came under the jurisdiction of the Venetian Republic. The older settlement developed on the peninsula and has retained its original Medieaval urban structure characterised by winding streets and small squares. Parts of the city defence walls fortified with towers dating to the XIVth century have been preserved. Because of dangers which always threatened from the sea the

Umag, the interior of the parish church of the Ascension of Mary (1730)

settlement gradually developed into the hinterland which offered fertile land especially good for the growing of vineyards. During the period of sudden tourist expansion Umag developed into a distinguished touristic destination with numerous hotels and facilities for sport and recreation.

The parish church of Mary's Ascension built as a one-naved church in the Baroque style during the first part of the XVIIIth century stands out among the preserved monuments. Its construction got under way in 1730. Like the other Istrian Baroque churches of the period it is characterized by a shallow cupola atop the sanctuary. It was built in the spirit of the Venetian Settecenta with many influences from new Classicist ideas. The church tower-shaped belfry was built as an independently-standing building. An organ dating back to 1776 can be found in the church and it has in its collection a part of the

Gothic polyptych from 1440. The church of St Pelegrine first mentioned as early as the XIIth century is found on Rožac bay.

A large countryhouse complex, the so-called "stancia" of the one time landowners of the region, can be found in the village of Seget not far from Umag. The main country house was built in the 18th century as a castle to which was attached a private chapel and lower husbandry buildings. These form a spacious square yard whose one side is entirely open to the holding. The architecture of the monumental cubic corpus of the central castle is harmoniously decorated with simple geometric ornamentation in the spirit of the late Baroque, imitating similar buildings of Venetian landowners on the Italian mainland. The front has a triangular gable supported by shallow cannelured pilastres in the spirit of Baroque Classicism.

Novigrad

Novigrad is located on a small peninsula which to the north encloses Tarski bay. This is the mouth of the river Mirna as it flows into the sea. In history it has been desig-nated a possible Greek colony; afterwards in Roman times the settlement Emmonia (Emona) was located on the broader locality of today's Novigrad. In the VIIth century

Novigrad, the three naved crypt under the sanctuary of the parish church of St Pelagio (VIIIth century)

during Byzantium rule it was called Neapolis (Civitas nova). It was during this century that the Slavs settled the area. From 1278 it was under the rule of Venice. Back in the VIIIth century Novigrad had become a see of a bishopric. It lost this designation in 1831. During the Venetian reign Novigrad was an important harbour for transporting wood and continued to be one up to the XVIIth century when it was destroyed by the Turks.

In earlier periods the historical center of the city was located on a small island which was connected to the mainland in the XVIIIth century by a broad embankment. Even today the old urban structure enclosed by walls with serrated battlements and two round towers has been preserved in relatively good condition. A number of valuable patrician homes and palaces from the period between the XVth to the XVIIIth century have been preserved in the city. Amongst these the palace of the aristocratic family Rigo dating from 1760 merits special mention. Today its first floor houses a collection of stone monuments with a rich assortment of Antique and Medieval monuments, especially those relating to the way the cathedral and its furnishings had originally looked like.

Today's parish church of St Pelagio is the former three-naved cathedral which was built in VIIIth century. During

the years 1746-1775 the building underwent an extensive renovation in the Baroque mode but it has partially retained its earlier construction. What has particularly been preserved is the three-naved crypt below the church sanctuary with cross vaults on columns. During the reconstruction in 1876 the last remnants of the portico in front of the church and the octogonal baptistry which was located to the south of the church facade were taken away.

In 1762 count Carlo Rigo built a very beautiful villa on his land in Karpinjan near Novigrad which bears witness to the refined taste and the high culture of the landowners.

One of the rare Istrian country complexes to be situated in the immediate vicinity of the sea was built in Dajla, somewhat to the north of Novigrad. This was the center of the land holdings of the Grisoni family. In 1775 count Santo Grisoni built two harmonious Baroque buildings which, joined as they are, form a yard. From this yard one exits through the decorated portal onto the seashore with a private small stone quay. A church was built on one of the longer sides of these buildings and on the opposite one an apartment for the chaplain. Both buildings have the same identical Baroque facade. At the beginning of the XIXth century count Grisoni erected at the rear end of the garden a representative building in the Classicist style with a trian-

The main altar of the parish church of St Pelagia in Novigrad (1749)

Novigrad, the bishop's seat in the parish church of St Pelagia

gular gable on the facade. The palace was projected by the French refugee, the architect Gabriel Le Terrier Du Manetote and built by the Kopar constructor Bracciaduro. This undertaking completed the architecture of this unique complex which bears witness to the wealth but also to the high culture of living of the upper social classes in northwestern Istria during the XVIIIth century.

Buje

If we leave the coastline of western Istria and head towards the interior of the region we will find ourselves on the hilly terrain of Gray Istria whose high grounds are dominated by picturesque small towns. Cultivated landscape, tilled earth and numerous vineyards, avenues of trees, groves and water courses are constituent parts of this exceptional area which many have compared to Toscany.

Buje, a town that grew on a rise of a hill from whence it spread with two of its wings to the neighbouring high grounds, is located in such a landscape, at the crossroads of important roads which from Pola lead to Trieste and from Umag to Buzet.

Buje developed on the location of a prehistoric hill-fort and numerous Antique findings from the Roman period indicate the settlement Nulle which antedated the construction of the Medieval city. The historical part of Buje has been preserved up to our days with its screen of narrow streets and walls with a Medieval tower. The walls were renovated in the XVth and the XVIIth centuries. Of the secular architecture one ought to emphasise the palace on the main square built in the style of the Venetian florid Gothic with a painted facade from the XVth century. A number of valuable patrician houses and palaces dating up to the period of the late Baroque can be found in the urban center of the city. A stone column from the XVIth century which has inscribed on it measures for length is located on the city square. The

Buje, view from the air

parish church of St Servola built in the XVIth century is also found there. It seems to have been raised on the location of some Antique temple because numerous Antique remains, especially parts of columns, steles and inscriptions were built into its walls. During the Baroque reconstruction in the XVIIIth century the original three-naved church was made

Buje, the interior of the parish church of St Servol (XVIIIth century)

into an edifice with one nave. The facade of the church has remained unfinished, lacking the decorative stone finish, so that it shows visible traces of built in Roman parts (spolium). Two valuable wooden sculptures of the Virgin Mary with the Infant from the XIVth and the XVth century are kept in the church. The belfry is separated from the church and dates back to the XVI century. The church of Blessed Mary located outside the city walls was built in the XVth century and preserves a high quality Gothic wooden sculpture of the Mother of God from the same period.

A museum with an ethnographic collection, particularly connected to olive growing, and with specimens of traditional crafts is also situated in the city.

New city neighbourhoods have risen around the old city. Today Buje is the administrative, economic and educational center of the wider region of Bujiština.

Right:
The lunette of the portal of the parish church of St Servol in Buje

Grožnjan from the air

Grožnjan

The Medieval fortified town Grožnjan grew on the high ground above the right bank of the river Mirna. Although the locality was inhabited in prehistory, the first mention of Grožnjan dates to 1103. Up to 1358 it was a fortified citadel in the possession of the Aquileian patriarch. From 1394 it was the possession of the Republic of Venice and became the center of its administration for the northern part of its lands in Istria. Grožnjan was surrounded by walls which were renovated in 1360 and 1367. The city gates made in the XVth and the XVIth century have been preserved. Originally they had a movable bridge. Alongside the gate inside the walls is a Renaissance loge from 1587. At one time above it was a "fondaco", a storage for grain. The parish church of St Mary, St Vid and St Modest is located on the main square. The church was built in 1770 on the remains of an older building from the XIVth century. The church houses a number of valuable articles, amongst these interesting choir benches from 1711 which leave a somewhat folkloris-

tic impression and with their motifs remind the viewer of the woodcuttings of Istrian folk coffers.

From the plateau in front of the church through the branches of centuries-old trees one has a beautiful view of the western part of Istria with the sea in the background. Many secular buildings from the period between the XVth and the XVIII century have been preserved in Grožnjan. The chapel of St Kuzma and Damijan built in 1554 and thoroughly renovated in the first part of the XIXth century is located in front of the city gates. The renowned Croatian painter Ivan Lovrenčić has recently painted its interior.

Although nowadays Grožnjan has only about eighty inhabitants it comes to life in the summertime with musical and artistic manifestations. In the organisation of the International Association of Musical Youth master competitions in the summer musical school are held here as well as numerous concerts. There are more than forty smaller gallery rooms and artistic workshops in Grožnjan.

Oprtalj, the interior of the confraternity church of St Mary with frescos by four masters from the second half of the XVth century.

Oprtalj

Not far away, in the vicinity of the Buje-Buzet road, on a high hill lies the fortified town Oprtalj. It was built on the site of a prehistoric hill-fort. During Roman times a military base was stationed there. In the Middle Ages Oprtalj was built as a fortified citadel. From 1209 it was under the rule of the Aquileian patriarch and from 1420 it fell under the power of Venice and remained so until the latter's demise.

The Medieval walls of the citadel have been partially demolished and a good part of these have been inbuilt into the town texture. In 1756 the town gates were entirely walled up. The Baroque town loge is found in front of them. The town square with the most important building of the parish church of St George is located in the center of the town. This is a Late Gothic church with three naves of ample dimensions and with a polygonal apse. The master from Kranj built it in 1526. The church has a number of valuable altars with images and a valuable Baroque bishop's mount with inlaid decorations. The church organ is the

31

The belfry of the parish church in Oprtalj

Oprtalj, view of the old town

*Right: Motovun, the main square. The parish church
of St Stephen was built at the beginning of the
XVIIth century while the Romanesque-Gothic
tower-belfry dates back to the XIIIth-XIVth century.*

Motovun

work of Gaetano Callido from the end of the XVIIIth
century. Oprtalj is also known for of its valuable Gothic
frescos. Frescos of the Kopar master Clerigino from the end
of the XVth century are to be found in the Romanesque
church of St Jelena. Frescos from the first half of the XVth
century can also be found in the church of St Leonard. The
confraternity church of St Mary from the XVth century is
the richest in wall paintings where alongside master Clerigino three anonymous XVth century painters made numerous frescos with scenes from the lives of Christ and the
Mother of God.

Opposite Oprtalj, on the left bank of the river Mirna, on
a steep rise (277 meters) overlooking the valley is picturesque Motovun. Like other Istrian settlements it was erected on the site of a prehistoric hill-fort. During the Middle
Ages it changed feudal lords and from 1278 it was under the
rule of Venice. Motovun had a strategically important position because from its heights it controlled the merchant
routes through the Mirna valley. Because of this during a
long period of its existence it was the communication center
of the entire area of continental Istria, especially for those
routes that lead to the seashore.

Motovun, the oldest part of the town

The town consists of three parts. At the very top of the hill is the oldest part surrounded by well-kept walls from the XIIIth and the XIVth century which in certain places are fortified with square defence towers. The entrance into this strongly fortified space is through the interior gate dating from the Gothic period. A suburb lies on the southern slope which was also fortified so that the south town gates from the XVth century were also built in the Gothic manner. The newest part of the town is the Gradicijol quarter which spreads over the extended eastern flank of the hill. The main town square is located at the juncture where the streets from this quarter come together between the old center of the town. On the north side is the Renaissance bastion with its town gates built in the first half of the XVIth century. The town loge from the XVIIth century is located on the plateau of one of the defence towers and leaves the impression of being a belvedere. The inner central town square is dominated by a Romanic-Gothic belfry-tower

Motovun surrounded by its vineyards famous far and wide

from the XIIIth-XIVth centuries on whose top is found a crenellated parapet. A monumental Renaissance palace-citadel which underwent alternations between the XVIth and the XIXth century is also found on the square. The spacious, one-naved parish church of St Stephen is a fine example of Late Renaissance Palladian architecture. It was built at the beginning of the XVIIth century. A large public cistern whose water-well parapets derive from the XIVth and XVth centuries is located below the main square.

Motovun is a place where many painters and sculptors gather and therefore it has many ateliers and small galleries. An international film festival has been held in this beautiful place during the last few years. It is also the seat of the International Center for Anthropology ICAM.

In its vicinity we find autochthonous woods of the common oak, elm-trees and ash-trees in which it is possible to find rare and exceptionally valued mushrooms - truffles. The Motovun region is also renowned for its vineyards and the production of high quality sorts of Istrian wine.

Buzet

The small town Buzet positioned itself almost in the center of the northern part of the Istrian peninsula, under the Ćićarija mountain range and in the immediate vicinity of the source of the river Mirna. Its favourable location accounts for the fact that it has been populated since prehistoric times. The Roman settlement on this site was known as Pinguentum. Significant necropolis of a number of civilisations have been found in the vicinity: a Langobardian graveyard from the beginning of the seventh century on Brežac hill and a Byznatium necropolis from the VIIth and the VIIIth century on the Mejica high ground. An Old Croatian burial site from the IXth and the Xth century was discovered in the immediate vicinity of the north town walls. From 1420 Buzet was under the rule of Venice and from 1511 it was the center of the military administrator of Venetian Istria. At that time Buzet was a strongly fortified town. Today there still remain preserved two gates built in the XVIth century.

The palace of the military administrator (Capitan de Raspo) stands out amongst the secular buildings. On the square, on its terrace sculpted from bedrock, rises the parish church of Mary's Ascension which received its contemporary shape by way of renovations in 1784. Since Buzet was a significant military and administrative Venetian stronghold it was very important to construct water storage systems. The town water storage system was renovated and given its contemporary shape in 1789 during the time of captain Marc Antonio Trevisani. This monumental construction with powerful Baroque volutes sculpted in stone wholly determines the architecture of the square. With its barrier and its stone bench it was not only the town's fountain but a place of socialising and resting in the very center of the town. Numerous exceptionally valuable and rich findings from the Buzet necropolises as well as the remains of the Roman Pinguentum settlement are kept in the town museum.

Draguć

The small town of Draguć situated itself to the southeast of Buzet on the road which leads towards Cerovlje and Pazin. It is a typical Istrian fortified settlement-citadel with a central square on which we find the parish church and the county palace. The Venetians built a cylindrical bastion in the XVIth century. What places Draguć apart are significant remnants of Medieval fresco painting kept in its two churches. All the walls of the small church of St Rocco, a building with one nave with a porch from the very beginning of the XVIth century, are covered with frescos painted by the Istrian painter the master from Padova between 1529 and 1537. The Frescos are particularly interesting as a compound of new Renaissance figurative ideas and the folk figurative expression.

Baroque water reservoir on the square in Buzet

Buzet from air

Roč

Amongst the numerous paintings the outstanding ones are the following: the homage of the three kings, the flight into Egypt and the Announciation. In the graveyard chaplet of St Elisia built during the Romanesque period (XIIIth century), Romanesque frescos with an emphatic Byzantium influence have been found. They show scenes from the life of Christ and the individual figures of the saints. The scene of the Announciation is painted on the triumphal arch.

The historical town Roč is located on an elevation dominating a fertile plain east of Buzet. In written documents from the XIth and the XIIth century it is mentioned as Ruz or Ronz. As in other examples of similar Istrian settlements one can record a continuity of life dating back to the Neolithic period. There was a significant settlement there during Roman times and was continued as seen by the findings of church architecture - the church of St Mauro and the

Hum, "the smallest city in the world"

baptistry from the Vth and VIth century. Only one tower on the northern side has been preserved from the Medieval citadel. The walls with their towers that have been preserved to our times were built after 1421 during the reign of Venice. Two layers of frescos were found in the apse of the chaplet of St Peter (St Rocco). The older layer represents a cycle devoted to St Paul and is the work of an unknown master from the XIVth century while the more recent layer is without doubt the work of a local Istrian painter from the XVth century and shows "Maiestas Domini" and the apostles. The parish church of St Bartholomew has undergone a number of alternations. Of interest is the Gothic sanctuary with a reticularly patterned vault added to the building in 1495. The church belfry was built at the beginning of the XVIth century. Parallel to the parish church stands the smaller church of St Anthony the Monk which was expand-

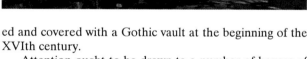

ed and covered with a Gothic vault at the beginning of the XVIth century.

Attention ought to be drawn to a number of houses of Renaissance contours but with a strongly emphasised rustical character. A Mannerist palace with a portico and the Baroque town loge (renovated in the XVIIIth century) are located on the square. The emphatically urban character which Roč retained through the centuries was lost with new buildings in the XIXth century.

From the XIIIth century Roč was a strong center of Glagolitic literature and the home of important Glagolitic writers such as Šimun Grebo, Žakan Jurij, Jeronim Greblo and Ivan Benčić. A number of Glagolitic books and collections of documents have been preserved to our days.

Above:
Hum, the belfry of the parish church of St Peter and Paul

Above left:
The lane of Glagolitic writers Roč-Hum, Želimir Janeš:
"The Table of Cyril and Method" (1978)

Hum

Owing to the emphatically urban character of its architecture and its organisation but also because of its miniature dimensions, Hum has received the epithet of "the smallest city in the world". It stands south of Roč and in the Middle ages it was referred to as Castrum Cholm. A sweep of walls spreads to the west while from the other sides the city is enclosed by an outer wall of interlocked houses. The city gate was erected in 1562 and near them is the belfry-tower from 1552. The parish church of St Peter and Paul has a Classicist facade that came into being after the renovation of 1802. The earlier church was built by master Gržinić in 1609. In the graveyard outside the city stands a small Romanesque one-naved church of St Jerome in which are to be found valuable paintings from the XIIth/XIIIth century evincing features of Romanesque art with a powerful influence of Byznatine artwork. The triumphal arch shows the scene of the Announciation, the southern wall shows the Advent while the north wall is decorated with a cycle of pictures showing Christ's Passion.

The lane of Glagolitic writers Roč-Hum, Želimir Janeš:
"The Rise of the Istrian Divide" nearby Hum (1980)

Hum was a strong Glagolitic center and from here derive Glagolitic codexes decorated with multicoloured initials.

The initiative of the Čakavian assembly in 1976 to plan an Alley of Glagolitic writers was soon realised. Scupture works on the local road between Roča and Hum symbolically mark the persons and events connected with the roots and the preservation of Slavic literacy. From 1977 to 1983 the famous Croatian sculptor Želimir Janeš constructed on 11 locations of this picturesque, seven kilometers long road symbolical stones markers in the open air. Going from Roč to Hum we meet the following markers: The Column of the Čakavian Assembly, The Table of Cyril and Methodius, The Chair of Kliment from Ohrid, The Glagolitic Lapidarium, The Gorge of the Croatian Lucidar, the Belvedere of Grgur

Poreč from air

from Nin, The Istrian Divide Highland, The Wall of Croatian Protestants and Heretics, the Resting Place of Deacon George, the Monument to Resistance and Freedom and the Hum City Gate which embellishes the calender with twelve medallions symbolically displaying the months of the year.

Poreč

The city of Poreč dominates the area from Tarski Bay on the north to Limska Cove to the south of the western coast of Istria as well as a significant part of the interior of the peninsula almost to its center point. This area is known as Poreština. Poreč is counted amongst the old cities and it is one of the historically and artistically most significant urban centers in Istria. The beauty of its monuments, especially the complex of the Euphrasian basilica, its value and significance is exceptional not only within the confines of Istria but also of Croatia and is numbered amongst the famous locations of the world's cultural heritage.

Poreč and its surroundings bear witness to remains of settlements from prehistoric times. During the Roman conquest of Istria the settlement on the peninsula and its harbour were deemed important and were turned into a castrum - a military base which shortly was promoted to the status of a municipality. From the second half of the Ist century BC the city acquired the rank of a colony under the des-

Poreč, fragments of the plastic ornaments of the Roman temple on the site of the onetime Roman forum

ignation Colonia Julia Parentium. Like all other Roman cities Poreč at that time acquired within its city walls the characteristic regular screen of streets which criss cross at right angles forming amongst themselves rectangular house blocs - "insulas". The main longitudinal street Decumannus runs in the east-west direction while the main transversal - the Cardo - vertically intersects it. The main city square, the Forum, is located in the westernmost part on the tip of the peninsula where in prehistoric times probably stood the cultic sanctuary. Even today one can see there the remains of the Capitol temple from the IInd century. Parts of the collonade which belonged to the peribolus of the capitol were found north of it. Although architecture changed, the basic distribution of Roman streets remained intact in the Middle Ages. Disregarding the irregularities that were caused by later additions and alternations it is still visible today. The

Poreč, the complex of the Euphrasian basilica. Floor mosaics of earlier date from the northern part of the basilica (Vth century)

shape and the length of the Roman defence wall did not change through the entire Middle Ages.

The first church space - the domus ecclesia - was located in a private house in the northern part of the city in the IIIrd century at the time when Christianity was still an illegal religion. Remnants of the mosaic floor with the symbolic motif of the fish belonged to this house. During the transition from the IIIrd to the IVth century Poreč became a bishopric. This is evidenced by an inscription from the end of the IVth century which narrates the transportation of the martyr's bones of bishop Mauro from the grave outside of the city into the area of the church. At that time the cult area was renovated and divided into two parallel rooms. One of them was dedicated to the cult of Mauro the martyr. The rooms were given new floors decorated with mosaics which have been preserved to our days. A huge basilica with three naves without

Poreč, the complex of the Euphrasian basilica. View of the roofing of the octogonal baptistry (VIth century)

an apse was built here in the Vth century. In the period between 535 and 550 bishop Euphrasius erected his own monumental building on the walls of the former. According to its architectonic conception but also going by the style of its mosaic paintings, the Euphrasian building was under the immediate influence of Byzantium art from the time of emperor Justian who, during the turbulent VIth century, tried to renew the unity of the Roman empire. Euphrasian basilica is three-naved and the aisles are separated from the central nave by pillars and arcading. Three apses are built on the eastern side of the building. The middle, deep halfcircle apse has outer polygonal walls while the two smaller side apses are also halfcircles but burrowed into the wall mass. The Euphrasian basilica is the earliest example of a three-naved church with three apses in the West. Each of the three apses was decorated. The capitals of the Euphrasian basilica belong to the typical Byzantium style while the preserved arches of the north arcading were decorated on the bottom

Poreč, the atrium of the Euphrasian basilica (VIth century)

by plaster decoration in relief. The mosaic works of this exceptional monument are its particular value. Only fragments showing a part of the composition of the apocalyptic Christ with the apostles have been preserved on the western facade of the building while the eastern facade shows the Transfiguration. The best preserved mosaics are those in the

45

Poreč, the Euphrasian basilica. Preserved original stucco-works from the VIth century on the vaults of the north arcades

central apse. Christ with the apostles is shown over the arch of the apse. The vault of the apse is decorated with a wide strip in which there are 13 medallions. The central one represents Christ in the form of the Mystic Lamb while the remaining 12 figures represent the 12 martyrs. The central scene in the half-cupola of the apse represents the Mother of God with the Child on the throne surrounded with angels and martyrs amongst which stands out St Mauro, the first

CLAVDI · EVERASI
VS   VS EPS
ARC

EVERASIV
S FIL
ARC

SCS MA
VRVS

*Poreč, the Euphrasian basilica. Images of bishop Euphrasius, archdeacon
Claudius and his son Euphrasius on the mosaic of the central apse (VIth century).*

bishop and martyr of Poreč. Next to him one sees the form of Euphrasius himself who in his hands holds a model of the church, then the archdeacon Claudius and the figure of the small boy Euphrasius, the archdeacon's son. The lower part of the apse displays extraordinary beautiful scenes of the Announciation and Visitation and the separate figures of Zaharia, the archangel Gabriel and St John the Baptist. The mosaics of the central apse of Euphrasian basilica, according to their quality, are considered to be amongst the most significant examples of wall painting during the VIth century throughout the world.

The lower belt of the apse is covered with very decorative multicoloured marble inscrustations. In the side apses one finds damaged mosaics which show the youthful figure

of Christ placing crowns on the heads of two martyrs: in the northern apse he is putting the crown on St Kuzma and Damjan and in the southern one on St Ursus and Severus.

The way the sanctuary looks today is the result of having the level of the floor in the central apse raised and the construction of a monumental ciborium decorated with mosaics dating from 1277. The recent reconstruction of the elements belonging to the altar railings have also contributed to its present appearance. Euphrasian basilica even as it appears today is an exceptionally harmonious building with elegant arcading and refined relations between space and the wall mass. Shining mosaics with a gold-plated background in the apses emphasise this harmony and focus the viewers attention on the space of ritual.

The vestibule of the basilica is connected to the spacious yard (atrium) which is surrounded by four porticos characterised by the same harmony and refined simplicity. An octoganal baptistry with a baptismal fountain has been erected on the western side. A belfry from the XVIth century leans on the external side of the baptistry. In the VIth century another three-naved church building was erected to the north of the Euphrasian basilica. This was probably

Left:
Poreč, the Euphrasian basilica. The apse of the main nave is ornamented with mosaics and marble incrustations from the VIth century. Down below in the middle is a ciborium decorated with mosaic over the main altar (XIIIth century)

Above:
Poreč, the Euphrasian basilica, a scene of the Announciation (mosaic in the central apse)

Right:
Poreč, the Euphrasian basilica, the scene of the Visitation (mosaic on the central apse).

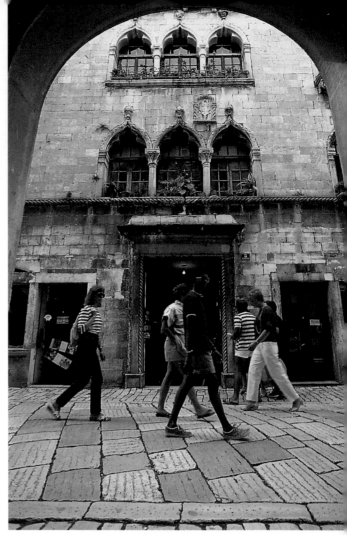

Poreč, Romaneque house with biforium and wood balcony

Poreč, Gothic palace in Decuman street (XVth century)

the church of St Andrew which was afterwards transformed into the bishop's residence.

A narrow corridor leads through the northern wall of the basilica to the memorial chapel from the VIth century. Its vestibule is elliptical in form while the chapel itself is tripartite. The outer wall of the vestibule and the chapel are polygonally shaped. The nearby sacristy was erected during the transition from the XIIIth to the XIVth century.

In 1251 a monumental Romanesque building, the residence of the canon, was erected to the south of the basilica in the Euphrasian complex. The architectonic decoration of this harmonious building consists of a beautifully shaped portal and a series of Romanesque distyles on the first floor.

In 1996 the entire episcopal complex in Poreč at whose core stands the Euphrasian basilica was added to the UNESCO list of world artistic heritage because of its exceptional multi-layeredness, the way it has been preserved and its exceptional artistic and historical significance.

A number of Romanesque and Gothic houses from the Medieval period have been preserved in the city center, especially at the crossing of the two main longitudinal and transversal streets. As far as Romanesque edifices are concerned, the interesting architecture of the two-storeyed building with a biforium and a wooden balcony on the main street has been preserved. The "House of Two Saints", so called because of its sculptures of St Kuzma and Damian which have been built into the facade, dates from the same period. The center of Poreč is endowed with a number of palaces from the XVth century built in the manner of the Venetian Gothic with an abundance of decorations and beautiful Gothic windows, especially triforia.

The preserved five-storeyed tower at the entrance into the city dates from the XIIIth century but was renovated between 1447-1448. The onetime Franciscan church dating from the end of the XIIIth century has experienced a strange fate. During the middle of the XIVth century it

Poreč, Gothic and Baroque houses on Matija Gubac Square

Poreč, Romanesque "House of Two Saints"

underwent alternations and enlargement. In the XVIIIth century Baroque stucco-works by G. Montevintia and illusionist paintings by A. Venturinia were added to it. In the second half of the XIXth century it was partitioned into two spaces, the more representative of which became the Istrian Assembly hall. Today it houses an exhibition space.

Poreč saw a lot of construction during the Baroque period. Among the wealthier buildings of the XVIIth and XVIIIth century we draw attention to the large Baroque palace of the Sinčić family, which today houses the local museum of Poreština, and the Zuccato palace. A large Baroque square with the large Late Baroque church of Our lady of the Angels built between 1747-1770 is located to the east outside the city walls. After the gradual demolition of the city walls during the XVIIIth century but especially in the XIXth century Poreč spread outside the perimeters of its walls and turned more and more of its representative facades to the sea.

Saint Lovreč Pazenatički, the municipal loggia located next to the south wall of the church of St Martin

Right: Saint Lovreč Pazenatički, the apses of the parish church of St Martin (XIth century)

The Poreč museum houses a collection of archeological findings, an etnographic and artistic collection and a collection of stone monuments. In 1974 the Collection of the Poreč Parish was set up which keeps a number of valuable examples of church furniture, paintings, vessels and mosaic fragments.

Poreč became a tourist center very early. The hotel "Riviera" was built as early as 1896. Its cultural wealth and the beauty of the city, in addition to its attractive surroundings with numerous bays, pine forests and tilled Istrian earth (bearing famous Istrian wines) has made Poreč into one of the most attractive tourist destinations not only in Istria but on the whole Croatian Adriatic coast. The numerous hotels, tourist settlements, camps and places of recreation which surround Poreč bear witness to this.

Sveti Lovreč Pazenatički

Sveti Lovreč Pazenatički is a smaller Istrian town located ten kilometers in the hinterland to the southeast of Poreč. The settlement dates back to the IXth century. The small

town stands on an oval ground map with two concentric streets. From 1304 to 1356 Sveti Lovreč was the center of the Venetian military administration in Istria while in the second half of the same century it was the base of the military commander for the Venetian territory south of the river Mirna ("paisanatico"). Today's walls with their partially preserved towers date from the Venetian period and were raised in the XIVth and XVth century. The well preserved south gate with the sharp Gothic arch dates from the same period.

The building which dominates Sveti Lovreč is the parish church of St Martin. This is a simply conceived early Romanesque three-naved building from the XIth century with three half-circle apses. Its interior is divided by arcadings supported by columns with characteristic Early Romanesque capitals. Two layers of frescos have been found in the northern and southern apses. The earlier date to the XIth century and alongside some features of Ottonian art display Byzantium influences. The later frescos are from the XVIth century and show the impact of Italian models. The harmonious simplicity and proportionality of the building is only disrupted by the rigid and imposing

Saint Lovreč Pazenatički from the air

western facade which was constructed during newer alternations which is not in harmony with the relatively small
free space in front of the church. On the other hand, to the
south the basilica is strongly attached to the surrounding
space by a spacious and harmoniously proportionate municipal loggia which leans on the southern wall of the church
and opens up towards the southern entrance onto the city
square. It today houses a rich collection of stones with monuments from Antiquity and the Romanesque period. In the
immediate vicinity of the church, behind its apses rises a
high and monumental belfry-tower which dominates the
eastern part of the settlement. The belfry has been constructed on the eastern entrance tower so that it has been
incorporated into the preserved cloak of city walls. A walled
up opening with a Gothic sharp arch very similar to the
town gate is clearly visible at the base of the tower. Stone
consoles of the defence balcony have been preserved above
it. High on the belfry the wall is disencumbered by use of
stone biforia of the Romanesque type and ends with a simple squarish crown covered with a wooden roof.

The church of St Lawrence whose side wall with stone
railed windows was built in early Romanesque times stands
in the graveyard. The simple belfry originated in the
Romanesque period.

Sveti Petar u Šumi

To the east of St Lovreč is situated the small village Sveti
Petar u Šumi which is famous for its large monastery complex. The Benedictine order built a monastery, whose buildings were of the Romanesque character, on that locality
around 1255. Around 1460 the monastery was taken over by
the Paulist fathers who kept it in use up to 1782 when the
church became a parish church and the monastery buildings
private property. The monastery and the church were
returned to the Paulists in 1993.

Very beautiful arcading with smooth capitals and sickle-
like arches have been preserved from the Romanesque complex. During alternations in the XVth and XVIth century
these were walled into the first floor of the monastery building while the ground-floor of the cloister was opened wide by
a series of Renaissance arches. Today's condition of the
monastery church of St Peter and Paul is the product of
alternations which the Paulites made at the end of the
XVIIth century and during the first half of the XVIIIth century. The narrow and steep Baroque facade of the church
completed around 1750 is similar to Paulite churches in
northern Croatia - in Lepoglava and Remeti. The belfry

Sveti Petar u Šumi, the facade of the Pauline monastery church of St Peter and Paul (1755)

which replaced the Romanesque one has features of similar Renaissance buildings. The interior outfit of the church with its altars and other church furniture is a unique stylistic whole, the work of the Paulite woodcutting workshop which was headed by the sculpter Pavao Riedl. He is the author of five stone sculptures within the facade niches. These works were made between 1755 and 1772. The altar paintings were made by the Paulite painter Leopold Keckheisen. The walls of the two chapels are panelled from base to cornice with decorative leather tapestry which are embossed with gold-plated patterns of large flowers, fruits and flowery branches. These are products of Venetian workshops from the end of the XVIIIth century and represent the most beautiful examples of such decorations in Istria. They give the church an especially sumptuous appearance reminding the viewer of the decorations in Baroque castles. The church organ was constructed by the master organ maker from Ljubljana Janez Juraj Eisel in 1770.

Sveti Petar u Šumi, the cloister of the Pauline monastery

Beram

Beram, the confraternity church of St Mary on Škrilinah

Only five kilometers to the west of Pazin on top of a hill lies the small and picturesque town of Beram. It rose on the site of an Illyrian hill-fort. The Medieval settlement was surrounded by a wall and defended by a strong rectangular tower. The parish church of St Martin was built in 1431 but was expanded and remodeled in the XIXth century. Numerous wall frescoes are visible within the church. The frescos in the sanctuary were made during the erection of the church by some master from upper Italy while those on the triumphal arch and showing St Michael and other saints and the angelic musicians (a fragment of the composition depicting the Holy Mother in Glory) were done by a Late Gothic master of the Venetian painting circle. A Late Gothic rustical relief of St Martin is kept in the church while the altar painting was done by the famous Croatian painter Celestin Mato Medović at the beginning of the XXth century. The graveyard and its confraternity church of St Mary on Škrilinah lies a kilometer northeast from the settlement. This is a Gothic one-naved building to which in the XVIIIth century was added a porch and the removed Gothic vault replaced by painted Baroque tabulas from 1707. The church is covered with Late Gothic frescos whose scenes are divided into 46 painted fields. As the signature on the frescos show they were painted by master Vincent from Kastav in 1474. At least two assistants had to help him in this enterprise. The longest composition is the Homage of the Three Kings which like a sumptuous tapestry runs eight meters across the northern wall of the church. The multitude of figures in the landscape present exquisite samples of the physiognomies of Vincent's contemporaries. Of equal importance is the composition showing the Dance of Death on the western wall where skeletal figures from different classes are entwined in a dance. The frescos of Vincent from Kastav derive from, on one side, the folk figurative tradition and, on the other, from refined international Late Gothic art. Because of their exceptional liveliness but also because of the Gothic idealism they embody these works are numbered amongst the most significant artefacts of Istrian wall painting.

Beram, the confraternity church of St Mary on Škrilinah. Fresco with scenes from the Dance of Death, the work of master Vincent from Kastav (1474)

Pazin

Pazinština is the area where all three Istrias, the White and the Gray and the Red, come together. The central position of this region on the Istrian peninsula has determined its importance so that the city of Pazin throughout history has always played a significant role. Today it is the administrative center of the Istrian county and the cultural, educational and economic center of continental Istria.

Throughout long centuries of its history Pazin was the feudal seat of the Pazin dukedom. It developed from the holdings of the Gorica dukes and spread out towards central Istria. In 1374 it became a possession of the Hapsburgs. The foundation of the feudal stronghold was the powerful Citadel built on a steep cliff over the Fojba, an abyss into which flows the Pazinčica, the only underground river in Istria. The Citadel which consists of four tracts organised around a central yard was first mentioned at the very end of the Xth century. The ground floor shows visible elements of Romanesque architecture while the rectangular tower was built in the XVth century. The contemporary appearance of the Citadel derives from 1537-1540 when the then landlords, the Moscon family, had the northern and eastern wing built. The Citadel was encircled by gullies and one made one's entrance through its five gates through a system of movable bridges. The system of gullies was filled in during the twenties of the XIXth century. From the XVth to the XVII century the houses and palaces of the prominent aristocrats were built in the immediate vicinity of the Citadel. The houses of the plebians and the craftsmen were built on the approach roads. The parish church of St Nicholas was built by the year 1266 and in 1441 received a spacious Gothic presbyterium with a star-like vault which was painted with extraordinary Gothic frescos around 1470. The size, the complex arrangement and the specific forms of the wall planes were obviously too

The central yard of the Pazin Citadel

Entrance into the Pazin Citadel

Center of Pazin from the air

demanding for the native Istrian masters. Probably after a recommendation voiced by the Pazin lords the task was taken by one of the painters from the circle of Jacob Sunter and he painted an exceptionally qualitative series of scenes of the Genesis (The Creation of the World), then the struggle of the good and evil angels with St Michael in the middle and scenes from the life of Christ with a Crucifixion scene.

The Parish church was definitively expanded and given a Baroque appearance in 1764. The marble Baroque altars stand out amongst the church furniture. The altar of St Nicholas has been attributed to the famous master Pasqual Lazzarini while the altar of our Rosy Mother to Antonio Michelazzi. The organs are the work of the famous Venetian organ maker Gaetan Callido from 1780.

The exhibition hall of the Etnographic Museum housed within the Citadel

The Franciscan church, expanded in the Baroque period, has retained its Gothic sanctuary from 1481. At the same time, during the nineties of the XVIIIth century, the east wing of the monastery was built. At the end of the XVIIIth century a grammar school and afterwards a famous secondary school was established in the Franciscan monastery in Pazin. Today the monastery prides itself with a very rich library and an archive.

The Citadel houses the Etnographic Museum of Istria with very rich collections of ethnographic objects and clothing and with a display of traditional crafts. A collection of old Istrian bells is situated within the museum.

Lindar

Lindar, a small Medieval town, dominates one of the hilltops some four kilometers distant from Pazin. It was first mentioned in 1379. Remnants of two half-cylindrical towers and the old belfry built on the foundations of the one-time tower have been preserved of the old city fortifications. The main city street leads to the square where the parish church

and the belfry completed at the beginning of the XXth century are situated. The votive church of St Sebastian and Fabian completed in 1531 is situated within the perimeters of the historical city.

The one-naved Gothic church of St Catherine, with its rectangular ground plan and with its characteristic Gothic vault, is located in front of the very entrance into the city. The church was painted with Gothic frescos typical for Istrian folk painting of the early XVth century. The best-preserved artefact is the so-called "Live Cross", a characteristic Late Gothic representation of the scene of Redemption. The date of composition of the fresco is recorded on the painted roll in Glagolitic letters - 1409. Traces of their Croatian Glagolitic inscriptions painted on similar rolls can also be made out on other frescos.

Gologorica

Gologorica is a small picturesque village to the east of Pazin. Its setup is typical for feudal Istria. To the east are the remnants of the wall with the main entrance gate which lead

Gračišće, view from the air

into the main street which broadens out onto the central square. The village is dominated by the church of Saint Peter built in the XVIIth century doubtlessly on the site of an older, Medieval building. The belfry is separated from the church. It houses artistic artefacts from the XVth century. The Gologorica church was erected with minimal

building resources as a collective folk effort and is one of the best examples to express the authentic needs of the ordinary Istrian populace. Only the Baroque marble altar, the votive gift of the De Franceschi family, later added to the church gives this place a feeling of Baroque sumptuousness.

The eastern Baroque facade of the country house belonging to the famous patrician family De Franceschi, with its balcony and portal, merits the visitor's interest. It was a part of the feudal homestead system and in large measure follows the conception of the famous Istrian "stancia".

The small church of St Mary, dating back without doubt to the Romanesque period, stands in front of the entrance to the village. It houses Gothic frescos made around 1400. The only scene that has come down to us is the Visitation of the Magi.

Gračišće, the porch of the church of St Mary on the Square with its Baroque wooden cassetted ceiling

The facade of the parish church of St Vid in Gračišće

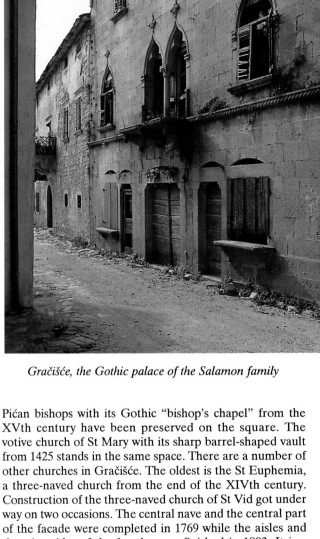

Gračišće, the Gothic palace of the Salamon family

Gračišće

Gračišće, another one of the fortified towns in the Istrian hinterland, is situated on a steep hillside not far from Pazin. Alongside the partially preserved Medieval walls and the town gates the cylindrical defence tower from the year 1500 has also been preserved. Gračišće is an especially interesting town because a number of representative buildings have been partially or wholly preserved within the perimeters of its walls. The municipal loggia from 1549, standing on the inner side of the entrance to the town, has been preserved. The most representative preserved building is the palace of the Salamon family dating to the XVth century. It is a harmonius stone Gothic palace with a characteristic Gothic biforium on the first floor. Remnants of the building complex which was the periodical seat of the

Pićan bishops with its Gothic "bishop's chapel" from the XVth century have been preserved on the square. The votive church of St Mary with its sharp barrel-shaped vault from 1425 stands in the same space. There are a number of other churches in Gračišće. The oldest is the St Euphemia, a three-naved church from the end of the XIVth century. Construction of the three-naved church of St Vid got under way on two occasions. The central nave and the central part of the facade were completed in 1769 while the aisles and the wing sides of the facade were finished in 1803. It is a well-elaborated Late Baroque building with a rich profilation and cornices and with a sumptuously polychromous marble altar in the sanctuary.

A series of artisan's houses from the XVI-XVIIth century with workshops on their ground floors have been preserved on the "Potok" locality in Gračišće while a series of houses from the XVth century with their characteristic arrangement - the cellar on the ground floor and a room on the first floor for living and an exterior stairway - have survived in "Pod Svetu Fumiju" street.

Pićan

The old town of Pićan has situated itself on a rocky height dominating the landscape. There is no doubt that the locality was inhabited in pre-historic times and during Roman times it was a military stronghold named Petina. The significance of this settlement in the past is confirmed by the fact that it was a bishopric from the Vth to the XVIIIth century. During the Middle Ages it was a Croatian settlement with a perfect at its head. The city was encircled by firm walls which were renovated throughout the Middle Ages. As time passed the walls were mutilated by the building of residences while the town gates dating from the transition between the XIVth and the XVth centuries have been preserved. The one time Medieval Pićan cathedral was thoroughly reconstructed during the Baroque period. The main nave was expanded in 1613 but the church was thoroughly modified in the Baroque spirit between 1720 and 1753. This is a decent three-naved church without excessive Baroque decorations which testifies to the difficult times and the humble circumstances of the Pićan bishops. The only true Baroque decoration is the altar, especially the main one where is located the altar palla of Valentine Metzinger from 1738 depicting the Announciation. The former Pićan seat is today the parish church of St Nikifor.

Not far from the town is the one-naved Romanesque church of St Michael with its half-circular apse. Its interior contains Gothic frescos from the first half of the XVth century especially on the northern wall. The scenes showing the Suffering of Christ, the Visitation of the Magi and the Last Judgement stand out as possessing special merit.

Žminj

Žminj is situated to the south of Pazin in the interior of the peninsula. The town was built on a height and was fortified with walls and cylindrical towers. Most of the fortification has been preserved. During the Middle Ages it was in the makeup of the Pazin dukedom. The parish church of St Michael built in the Baroque style is situated on the spacious city square. Its interior houses a rich Baroque inventory, especially valuable altars and pulpits. The one-naved space of the church has been built upon with a series of chaplets on both sides so that one gets the impression that the church is three-naved. The addition of the chaplets got under way in the first half of the XVIIth century and the church with its present appearance and its facade was com-

pleted in 1717. The church with its representative dimensions and its plastically rich facade defines the square in a powerful manner. The rich vegetation encircling it highlights its Baroque appearance.

The small Gothic chaplet of the Holy Trinity leaning on the parish church contains valuable Gothic frescos that were made, according to the inscription, in 1471. Going by stylistic characteristics, the master who painted the 31 scenes from the life of Christ belonged to one of the Slovene workshops. The wall pictures in the chaplet have suffered noticeable damages.

The small yet harmonious congregationist church of St Anthony the Monk is situated within the city proper. This is a one-naved simple church covered by a pointed vault. According to the inscription on the facade it was erected by master Armirigus in 1381. It houses a series of high-quality but damaged frescos which without doubt belonged to some Venetian master from the end of the XIVth century. The apse has a well preserved scene of the Crowning of the

Žminj, detail of the fresco in the chapel of St Anthony

Žminj, Baroque parish church of St Michael

Mother of God. The vault displays scenes from the life of St Anthony the Hermit while the wing niches show scenes from the life of Christ.

In the fifties an important Early Croatian necropolis, with graves from the IXth and the XIth centuries, was found not far from Žminj.

View from the sea of Vrsar and its harbour

Right: Lim bay, view from the air

Every year in Žminj on St Bartholomew's day (August 24th) there is massive folk festivity which attracts a large number of people from the vicinity but also from the whole of Istria.

Vrsar

Returning to the western coast of Istria we find ourselves in Vrsar on the very edge of Poreština, north of the Bay of Lim. The town of Vrsar is located in a very picturesque landscape. The hill on which the settlement rose falls to the bay before which is a number of green islets. This space was favourable to habitation since prehistorical times so that remains of Illyrian hill-forts are to be found on the surrounding hills. Remnants of seaport constructions, a large villa rustica and a quarry have been found alongside the seashore dating back to Roman times. In the Vth century a large Old Christian sacral complex was formed in the settlement of Ursaria and was wholly demolished during the Slav-Avarian inroads into Istria. Only high-quality floor mosaics with figural motifs have been preserved. During the Middle Ages Vrsar was a fortified settlement and the center of the feudal holdings of the Poreč bishops. A citadel was built on the hill at that time. The three-naved church of St Mary of the Sea built in the XIIIth century dates from the Romanesque period.

Owing to its picturesque location this one time settlement of fishermen and wine-growers has emerged as a very powerful and cherished touristic destination in western Istria.

The Bay of Lim

The Bay of Lim is an unusaul geomorphological phenomenon created by the flooding of the lower part of the Cove of Lim and its becoming a 10 kilometers long and a 500 meters wide sea bay whose shores steeply rise into the heights of more than a hundred meters. Gradually narrowing towards the interior it becomes the dry Kraska valley which up to Kanfanar lies in a east-west direction to suddenly verge towards the north up to within 5 kilometers of Pazin. The stream Lim periodically flows through the valley. It is probable that this Kraska phenomenon was created by

the once existent flow of the river Pazinčica which today is an underground river. The total length of this valley together with the bay is over 35 kilometers. Throughout the centuries the long Kraska valley was the main direction in which the entire traffic from the western coast of Istria towards its interior took place. The Bay of Lim itself is a very picturesque bay whose shores are overgrown with evergreen vegetation and is today a touristic attraction. Fisheries and shell beds are located in its upper part.

In the past the bay of Lim was inhabited as far back as the Neolithic period so that numerous caves with traces of life are to be found along its shore. On both of its sides hillforts were constructed in Illyrian times of which the most prominent one is the one over the southern shore on the hill of St Martin. In Antiquity the border - "lime" - passed through this space, dividing the region of Poreč from Pola. The Latin term has bequeathed the present day name to the bay. On the northern shore is the famous Romualdo's cave where, according to legend, lived the hermit Romualdo in the XIth century, the founder of the Benedictine monastery of St Michael. The ruinous remnants of this important construction from the Early Romanesque period are to be found high above the northern shore of the bay. At the southern side of the entrance into the Bay of Lim is situated the three-naved church of St Euphemia with three rectangular apses in the sanctuary.

Dvigrad

Dvigrad represents today the ruinous remnants of the fortified Medieval settlement which rose above the Cove of Lim. In Illyrian times there were two hill-forts which dominated the surrounding hills. In the early Middle Ages they were called Parentino and Moncastello. The first went out of existence very early while the latter developed into the Medieval town bearing the name of Duecastelli - Twocity. It was the possession of the Aquileian patriarch and later of the Venetian Republic. Life continued there up to 1631 when the city was devastated by the plague. The survivors found shelter in nearby Kanfanar. Besides the partially preserved walls and towers the structure of the Medieval town, with the partially preserved walls of more than 220 houses, is clearly visible. The ruins of the three-naved Romanesque basilica of St Sophia built in the XIth and the XIth century on the site of an older building are located at its center. In the graveyard under the hill of the ruins of Dvigrad, alongside the road Kanfanar-Mrgani, stands the one-naved Romaesque congregationist church of St Mary of Lakuč in which are found frescos from the third quarter of the XVth century. These were made by the Late Gothic Istrian painter, the so-called "Mottled Master". It is obvious that the same master also painted the frescos in the small church of St Anthony before the very entrance into Dvigrad.

Kanfanar

Kanfanar, situated on the other side of the Cove of Lim began to develop as a town in the XVIIth century when the inhabitants of Dvigrad, taking refuge before the plague, moved in. At the beginning of the XVIIIth century the early Gothic stone pulpit from the XIIIth century with a relief of St Sophia holding two cities in her hands, the painted doors from the XVIth century and a number of wooden

The site of Dvigrad over Lim Cove

sculptures were transported from the Dvigrad basilica into the parish church of St Sylvester (XVIIth century).

Two kilometers north of Kanfanar alongside the road is situated the village of Barat with its pre-Romanesque one-naved church of St Agatha from the XIth-XIIth century in which are to be found one of the earliest preserved Istrian Medieval frescos. They are of the early Romanesque character with a strong influence of Byzantine art and were created probably at the same time as the completion of the church.

69

Rovinj

On the indented coast with numerous coves and smaller islands, to the south of the Bay of Lim, lies Rovinj one of the most beautiful and picturesque cities on the Adriatic coastline.

The situatedness of the historical core of the city of Rovinj on a smaller peninsula which stretches itself into the sea between two deep coves contributes to the atmosphere of spatial harmony. The steep buildings of the old city, which almost from sea level climb towards the top of the hill, form a homogeneous tissue of picturesque, narrow and winding streets huddled on the hill like a clenched fist. The long horizontal of the parish church, partially softened by the greenery of the trees, dominates the high hill and the final compositional accent is imprinted by its monumental belfry pro-

ery surrounding the city. In this way the feeling of architectonic fullness and completeness of the greater city center has been preserved. The logic of change of styles in the urbanistic plans and the conceptions of expanding the city can clearly be traced. The green forested island of St Catherine imprints upon the southern Rovinj inlet a particular atmosphere.

Like other Istrian cities Rovinj is a very old settlement. It rose on an island which was separated from the land by a tiny strait. According to the records of an anonymous scribe from Ravena from the VIIth century a Castrum Rubini had existed on the site for a very long time, probably already by the IVth century.

The Roman castrum was probably located on the site of today's parish church of St Euphemia and the nearby graveyard. During Roman rule the Rovinj region was thickly populated which is corroborated by numerous country houses - villa Rustica. On the nearby island of St Andrew glass was produced so that not long ago the island was strewn with glass shards. In the early Middle Ages Rovinj was mentioned under a number of names: Ruvigno, Ruino, Ruginio, Revigno. The peaceful Roman period was followed by turbulent times when different peoples made inroads and war campaigns from land as well as pirate sea attacks endangered the space of Istria. From the VIth to the Xth century many refugees from central Istria sought shelter on the fortified Rovinj island so that the settlement developed into a typical Medieval city. The importance of Rovinj as a city center can be seen in the fact that its representatives participated in the the work of the Rigano assembly in 804. During the period of the feudalisation of Istria feudal lords were constantly changing while the coastal Istrian cities led an incessant battle for municipal autonomy. It became particulary acute during the reign of the Aquileian patriarchs. The

truding high into the sky. The vertical lines of the high buildings are enforced by the numerous picturesque high chimneys adorning the rooftops of Rovinj.

The old city is separated from the newer quarters by an isthmus where crisscross a number of spacious Baroquely defined squares and streets built in the belt before the city walls and on the space which was partially created by filling in the sea. The newer parts of the city built in the XVIIIth and the XIXth century spread out harmoniously like a fan onto the two Rovinj inlets or climb up the opposite hill which is dominated by a complex of Franciscan monasteries. The newest city quarters built in the second half of the XXth century as well as the complexes of tourist accommodations are located relatively far from the old urban core and are partially submerged into the luxuriant green-

Rovinj, picturesque Baroque houses on New Square

agreement between Rovinj and Dubrovnik from 1188, obliging both sides to engage in mutual trade and exchange of goods, is an interesting development of that time.

Between the growing presence and strength of Venetian power on the one hand and the administration of the Aquileian patrirachs on the other, Rovinj, like other Istrian coastal cities, gave its support now to this now to that side trying to attain its own privileges. In 1310 it definitively went over to Venice. The Venetian administration formally left Rovinj with communal freedoms but retained the right to install its podesta under whose jurisdiction fell all the activities significant for the life of the city. Since the Venetian economy was primarily turned to trade the one-time Istrian holdings stagnated while the cities saw the emergence of new occupations - craftsmen, merchants and seamen. The population of Rovinj greatly expanded during the Turkish incur-

The largest square in Rovinj, Marshal Tito Square

sion into the West. Numerous refugees from Dalmatia and Bosnia but from Albania and Greece as well settled the areas of western Istria. The Venetian administration issued a permit to a group of herdsmen to settle the pastures nearby Rovinj and in 1525 they established the Rovinj village. With the multiplication of the city population a twofold parallel process got under way. There was less and less space in the city enclosed within its walls so that existing houses were built upon one or two storeys or more. In such a manner Rovinj became a city of very tall buildings (three and four storeys). On the other hand, with the waning of the danger of attack by potential enemies, more and more houses were built outside the city walls. The first to be built was a series of buildings between the inner and outer defence wall and a new, large square was formed on the waterfront (Piazza della Riva). Under pressure from the Franciscans the settlement of the land on the hill around the Franciscan monastery got under way. Finally when immediate threats of war disappeared in the middle of the XVIIIth century the

stone bridge was taken down and the canal that separated the Rovinj island from the main was filled in so that the city began to spread freely on the surrounding area. At the end of the XVIIIth century Rovinj almost had 10.000 inhabitants, a significant production of agricultural goods, a developed fishing industry and shipping. The high quality stone quarried in the vicinity of Rovinj was the material from which many important buildings in Venice, Padova, Ancona and elsewhere were built. Allegedly, the famous Venetian church of Santa Maria della Salute was made out of Rovinj stone.

A harbour in the northern cove and a breakwater in the south cove facing the island of St Catherine were built during the period of Austrain rule. Industry began to develop on the outskirts of Rovinj during the second half of the XIXth century. Amongst other industries the most prominent is the large tobacco factory established in 1872. The essential fact dictating the investor's choice was the large number of unemployed women in Rovinj and its surroundings. In

Rovinj, Baroque Califfi palace which today houses the Rovinj Museum

accordance with the great fishing tradition an important factory for canning fish was established in 1882. From 1873 Rovinj was connected by railroad via Kanfanar. After WWII, but particularly after the sixties, tourism underwent a period of rapid development. Complexes of hotels, touristic and camp settlements encircle the broader region of Rovinj and its islands. Because of its natural attractions but particularly because of its picturesque and valuable historical environment, Rovinj is one of the most attractive tourist destinations on the Croatian coast. Lately, more and more attention has been given in Rovinj to nautical tourism.

The cultural and historical heritage of Rovinj is very significant. It need be said that unlike Poreč and Pola Rovinj does not possess individual architectonic monuments of world significance but what makes Rovinj exceptional in the company of the other cities is its entirely pre-

The County Museum in Rovinj, collection of artworks from XVIth to the XVIIIth century

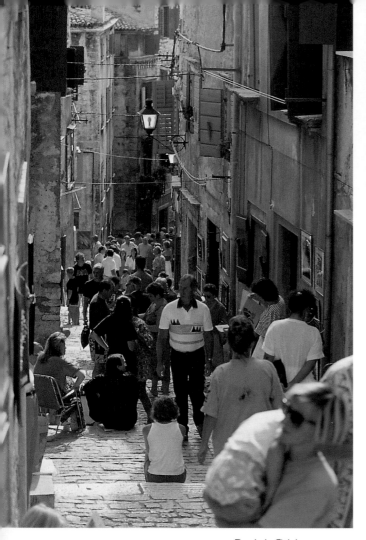

Rovinj, Grisia street   *A scene from old Rovinj*

served urban core. It developed naturally and was built up through the centuries under different influences, mirroring the unbroken history of the city. Unscathed by war, preserved unlike Pola and Poreč from the horrible destructions of WWII, Rovinj, alongside the integrality of its urban space, has preserved its precious ambient values, its picturesqueness and its unique, almost natural, organic makeup.

The old urban core on the former island consists of compact irregular blocs of buildings or huddled series of houses alongside narrow streets. In the space behind the onetime main city gates (the place where the vault Balbi today stands) was situated the main square of St Damjan (today Matteoti square). From this square or its vicinity the main city communications, the streets Trevisol, Montalbano, Garzotto, Grisia, Casale, Zdenac and Silvano spread out in the form of a fan. In their broken stride they climb towards the plateau on the top of the hill. A whole series of smaller and

winding streets and passageways crisscross these main arteries forming an almost capillary-like system of communication between the tall buildings. At a number of points small, frequently irregular squares are formed like outlets for catching air in the swarming city tissue (Pian del Tibio, Old or Large square, "The Star"). The old core of Rovinj is charcterised by numerous vaulted underpasses - sotoportici - which open passageways between particular streets or through blocs of houses. These are generally covered with vaults although there are more simple ones with a flat covering. The system of these underpasses frequently creates picturesque broad spaces such as the one called "The Field on the Hill" or interesting sites such as "Under the Vaults". The Rovinj underpasses are not mere passages or communication venues but residential quarters are built over them which contributes to the picturesque quality of the environment. As the streets rise towards the hill Rovinj abounds in numerous stair cases. The original stone pavements of the city streets add a particular value to the environment. The stone set in "fish bones" patterns merits special mention because of its decorativeness. The onetime Rovinj fortification are today hard to make out because houses have been partially built into them and in large measure they have been demolished. Only one rectangular tower in V. Švalbe street, remade into residential quarters, has been preserved. Three of the four city gates can still be seen.

No prominent Medieval buildings are to be found in the old part of the city. A characteristic Gothic window is visible here or there but the majority of the architectonic decorations disappeared during alternations and the building of upper storeys during the Late Renasissance and the Baroque period. Of Renaissance buildings the two harmoniously built palaces which flank Montalbano street at the point where it opens up onto the Old Square ought to be mentioned. They stand out with their finely treated stone bloc structure and with the precious modulation of the window openings. On the second storey both have an impressive Renaissance stone balcony with balusters. Both buildings accentuate the western part of the square. Going by the date engraved on one of the entrance portals they were built in 1580.

The Baroque period was a time when much was built and alternated in Rovinj but it is difficult to find within the old city core a building which was systematically built according to the taste and measure of the Baroque. It is easier to find isolated examples of characteristic Baroque portals or stone balconies with profiled parapets and pear-like balusters. The most significant integral and monumental Rovinj Baroque palace Califfi (today it houses the Local Museum of Rovinj) is situated on the square before the city walls where the Baroque concept of the palace could evolve in adequate environs. Within the city walls on Matteoti square is situated the palace of the Venetian podesta (today housing the city administration) which was alternated at the close of the XVIIth century. What especially stands out on this building is the monumental portal with doorjambs whose decorativeness and monumental impression are founded on the contrast and alternation between the larger, unfinished, roughly-cut stone parallelepipeds with smaller finely-cut ones. Over the gate is a level epistyle and a cornice with a coat of arms and a shield in the middle.

Old Rovinj, Poljana on the hilltop

Rovinj, the main facade of the parish church of St Euphemia

Rovinj, the interior of the parish church of St Euphemia

Nearby is found the decorative Baroque vault Balbi placed there in 1680 on the site of the onetime eastern city gate. In its lower part the vault is built out of large stone parallelepipeds and its keystone has on both its sides a large and somewhat rustic marble head. The attic crowning the vault carries two joint-like scrollworks and a folded gable with a central decorative vase. The coat of arms of the podesta and the Venetian lion of St Mark are situated within this decorative Baroque complex.

With its tall, narrow facades and streets which spread from it in a ray-like fashion, the New Square in front of the new city quarters represents another picturesque setting.

The most significant Baroque complex in Rovinj is without doubt its large parish church of St Euphemia (Fume). In order to build a church of such large dimensions on the plateaue overlooking the old city it was necessary to tear down the late antique church of St George and two other buildings - the churches of St Ursula and St Michael. The first building that was erected was the monumental tall belfry modeled on the one standing on the square of St Mark in Venice. The belfry was built between 1654-1680 accord-

ing to the plans of the architect Manopolo. A bronze sculpture of St Euphemia, the work of the brothers Vicenzo and Bisto Vollani, was placed at its top in 1758. The large three-naved church of St Euphemia was built between 1728-1736 according to blueprints made by the Venetian architect Giovanni Dozzi. The interior of the church is characterised by its height and monumentality expressed through the high arcading and above it a strong, finely profiled cornice. The three main altars, the central one and the two wing altars of the Holy Sacrament and of St Euphemia have been placed on the same level which endows each of the naves of the church with a certain independence. A Baroque rhythm has been achieved through a certain longitudinal tension directed towards the center. The sanctuary and the choir of the church are decorated with rich stucco-works by the Venetian master G. Lattuga from 1750. All three altars were planned by the famous Venetain altar maker Girolamo Laureto in 1741 while the sculptures overhanging them were done by one of the most renowned Venetian sculptor of the time Alvise Tagliapietra, a representative of the Venetian Rococo. To complete this large commission he was assisted

The statue of St Euphemia (XVth century) in the Rovinj parish church bearing the same name

The Bronze statue of St Euphemia placed in 1758 on the top of the belfry of the parish church in Rovinj bearing the same name

by his sons Ambrogio and Giovanni. The church also contains the large uncompleted Antique sarcophagus from the IInd-IIIrd century which once belonged to the torn down Late Antique church of St George. The stone panelling of the wing facade was put up according to blueprints made by the architect Simon Battistella while the main facade was completed in 1883 according to the plans of engineer Depozza.

On the rise in the new part of the city on the mainland the Franciscans built the simple Baroque church of St Francis in 1702. Next to it an observatory was erected which in 1746 was transformed into a monastery. A valuable heptagonal Romanesque chapel of the Holy Trinity with a cupola is situated on the Lokva locality in the southeastern part of the newer city quarters (not far from the present bus terminal). This is the oldest preserved sacral building in the area of Rovinj. Of interest on this building is the stone-railed

window on which is engraved the scene of the Crucifixion with the Holy Mother, St Peter and two of the apostles.

Worthy of special interest amongst the other sacral objects in Rovinj is the church of St Mary of Kindness from the XVIIIth century, one of the most beautiful Baroque churches in the southern part of Istria. A porch characteristic for the Istrian region was added to it in 1750 but was erected in the Classicist spirit with a triangular gable and raised upon seven steps as though it were some kind of Antique temple.

Showing an uncommon and refined sense for environmental values the Rovinj tobacco factory carefully restored its production halls according to the original design. At the same time it contributes to its surroundings with valuable horticultural solutions. Owing to this we can sightsee handsome examples of industrial architecture from the last quarter of the XIXth century. The factory halls were built between 1873-1875 while the administrative building was completed in 1909.

On Zlatni rat, the peninsula which closes off the harbour of Rovinj on its southern side, a large English-styled sort of park spreads out with very emphatic perspectival solutions. The park abounds with rare examples of Mediterranean flora. A group of high cedars are particularly beautiful. The old Muntrav quarry is situated within the environs of the park. Stone from this quarry went into the covering of many famous Venetian buildings.

Remains of Antique architecture are visible in the shallow waters of the nearby island of St Andrew (Red island). A Benedictine monastery has stood there since the VIth century. In 1420 it was taken over by the Franciscans who remained there up to 1820. A part of the monastery and the central part of the pre-Romanesque church were incorporated in the XIXth century into the complex of the Hutterot private villa (today a part of the newly-built hotel). Within the one-time church we find today a smaller collection of stone statues from the XVth and the XVIth century.

The large Baroque palace Califfi in Rovinj houses the County Museum. Its permanent display contains a very valuable collection of paintings from XVI-XVIIIth century as well as a rich collection of contemporary art. The ground floor of the Museum stages occasional museum exhibitions as well as showings by contemporary artists.

Every summer artists who live in Rovinj organise in Grisia street a one day exhibition of their works out in the open.

Rovinj, Romanesque chaplet of the Holy Trinity

Svetvinčenat

The interesting town of Svetvinčenat is situated on a woody high ground to the east of Rovinj in the hinterland of Istria alongside the Pula-Pazin road. The uniqueness of its urban architecture is based on the quadrilateral Renaissance square in the center of the town which is enclosed by the facade of the parish church, the municipal loggia, a number of Renaisance houses and the Morosini-Grimani citadel. A water collector with a water-well crown is found at the center of the square. The building which absolutely dominates this space is the large and monumental Grimani citadel. It was built as a rectangular fortress with

Svetvinčenat, view from the air

cylindrical towers in its corners and a simple facade. During the XVth century the citadel was the property of the Morosini family who extended the Medieval fortress and reconstructed it in the forms of the late Renaissance. The same family built other public edifices on the square. In the XVIth century the citadel became the property of the Grimani family who at the end of the same century made certain alternations. The facade which is turned to the square is characterised by a tall rectangular tower with a roof and a powerful three storeyed building whose only decoration is a powerful final cornice with a series of decorative consoles. A monumental entrance gate is to be found in the high wall connecting these two buildings. The other two corners of the citadel are protected by cylindrical Medieval towers. The Morosini-Grimani citadel in Svetvinčenat is the best preserved in Istria.

A very spacious and monumentally conceived municipal loggia with very elegant arcading whose vaults are decorated on the interior side is located on the opposite side of the square. The loggia has two entrances, one opening onto the square, the other onto a sidestreet.

The parish church of the Announciation was built at the transition from the XVth into the XVIth century and has a typical Renaissance trefoiled facade. Within it is kept the painting "Mary and the Saints", probably the work of the Venetian painter Palma the Younger.

The church of St Vincent, a one-naved Romanesque church with three apses which probably used to belong to some abbey, is situated at the graveyard. It has preserved three layers of frescos of which only traces remain of the oldest layer. The second layer derives from the XIIIth century and was painted by master Ognobenus from Trevis. The frescos are of the Romanesque character with strong influences from Byzantine painting. As far as its size is concerned this is the largest cycle of Romanesque frescos in Istria. The third, earliest layer of wall paintings belongs to some Italian master from the second half of the XIVth century or from the very beginning of the XVth century.

The square in Svetvinčenat. To the left is the rectangular tower of the Morosini-Grimani citadel, to the right the Renaissance parish church of the Announciation

Svetvinčenat, the Morosini-Grimani citadel

Bale, the Soardo-Bembo citadel with Gothic quadroforia (XIVth-XVth century)

Bale

The picturesque town of Bale lies on a lonely hill half way between Rovinj and Vodnjan. The Medieval settlement rose on the site of a onetime hill-fort and a Roman castrum. Its most important architectonic complex is made up of the Soardo-Bembo citadel created by joining two earlier towers having rectangular groundplans with a central residential tract decorated by Gothic quadriforums. The tract was built during the years of transition between the XIVth and the XVth century. The entire complex of the citadel leaves a monumental and powerful impression on the viewer. Of the profane architectue in Bale attention ought to be drawn to the municipal loggia, the pretorian palace and the fondaco (grain

Bale, the parish church of St Julian and Romanesque belfry

Bale, entrance into the Soardo-Bembo citadel

storage place). The large parish church is of recent date and was built in 1880, while the model for its construction was the late Baroque parish church in Vodnjan. The church was built on the site of the three-naved basilica from the Old Christian period. The monumental self-standing belfry of the parish church shows features of the Romanesque manner. The church houses a sarcophagus with pre-Romanesque reliefs and a collection of wickerwork plastic is to be found in the crypt. The church possesses a valuable wooden Romanesque crucifix and the large painting "The Visitation" has been attributed to the painter Matteo Ponzoni. In the town itself and in its immediate vicinity are to be found other smaller churches from the XIIIth-XVth century. Some years ago bones of the brontosaur, a gigantic reptile of the dinosaur family, were found on the littoral near Bale which is one of the rare Paleonthological finding in Europe. The discovery of this gigantic animal initiated the idea of founding a paleonthological collection in Bale.

Peroj

The old Istrian village of Peroj, first mentioned at the beginning of the IXth century in connection with the Rižan assembly, is located west of Vodnjan, in the valley somewhat distanced from the sea. The settlement was abandoned after one of the severe epidemics of the plague. In 1658 it was settled by colonialist who had come from Montenegro. The Orthodox parish church of St Spiridon safekeeps the Cretean-Venetian icons transported from the Orthodox church of St Nicholas in Pola. At the edge of the settlement stands the old church of St Stephen which shows a mixture of elements of late Antique and Byzantine-Ravenian architecture. The facade is subdivided with four pilasters.

Nearby Peroj in the field leading towards Mandriol in the immediate vicinity of the village of Batvači is situated the small three-naved Basilica of St Foška with three

Church of St Foška near Peroj

engraven apses. The church was erected in the VIIth century and underwent alternations in the XIIth and again in the XVIth and the XVIIth century. The location of the building alongside the long-used Roman road made the basilica a place of pilgrimage so that in the XVIth century a spacious porch was constructed for the needs of the pilgrims. At one time the whole interior of the church was painted whereas today only fragments in the apses remain. The best preserved is the representation of the Ascension of Christ on the triumphal arh over the central apse. This is an excellent example of the high quality Romanesque Benedictine wall painting from the XIIth century.

Vodnjan

Ten kilometers north of Pola stands Vodnjan one of the most significant and the biggest urban centers of southern Istria. Encircled by olive groves and vineyards nourished by the rich Istrian soil, Vodnjan climbs a gentle slope. Its recognisable characteristic is the monumental urban structure and especially the tall belfry of its parish church rising into the skies.

Vodnjan was first mentioned in the middle of the XIIth century as Atinianum. At the beginning of the XIVth century a citadel with ditches and defence towers was built on its western side. It was torn down in 1808. The Medieval settlement formed near the top of the slope constructing a complex of narrow streets with covered underpasses and huddled houses. A number of handsome examples of Gothic profane architecture (the Bettica palace) are to be found in such an environment. Newer parts of the city were built during the XVIIth and the XVIIIth centuries alongside both sides of the broad, so-called Merchant street. On its left and on its right side this street is made up of a series of tall, frequently three-storeyed buildings with stores or artisans's workshops on the ground floor. Near the top Merchant street gradually narrows onto the spacious Vodnjan main square encircled by a row of valuable and interesting buildings.

Vodnjan, late Baroque church of St Blaise (1760-1800)

The parish church of St Blaise is situated on its own, separate square. It was built during the late Baroque period on the site of an earlier pre-Romanesque church. The construction got under way in 1761 and the church was consecrated in 1808. Its dimensions - 56 meters in length, 32 meters wide and 25 meters high - make it the largest parish church in Istria. The belfry, 62 meters high, was completed only in 1882. The building of the Vodnjan parish church was in those days an accomplishment equal to the construction of the complex of St Euphemia in Rovinj. For years the construction was under the direction of architect Domenico Dongetti from Piran and as its model it probably had the church of San Pietro in Castello in Venice. The church is three-naved. Three intercolumns connect the wing aisles with the main nave into a single, very imposing space. The transept is the same height as the main nave and the cupola rises over the crossing. The atmosphere of Baroque unrest is particularly noticeable within the space of the sanctuary.

A collection of sacral art containing a series of valuable artefacts from the XIVth to the XIXth century was opened in 1984 within the parish church building complex. Prominent amongst these are the polyptych of the Blessed Leon Bembo from 1321, the work of the famous Venetain painter Paolo Veneziano, and the Renaissance triptych of the Blessed Leon Bomba, the work of Lazar Bastiani from the XVIth century. Over a hundred different reliquaries are to be found amongst the collection. The largest part of this valuable collection of artefacts was brought from Venice to Vodnjan in 1818 by the painter Gaetano Gresler. He gathered the collection together in different ways, chiefly by saving discarded artefacts during the demolition of churches under Napoleon's rule but also by buying things from the French soldiers.

The Vodnjan parish church offers a special attraction in its series of well-preserved mummified bodies of saints and blessed persons. The tissue on the mortal remains of St Nikoloza from Kopar who died in Venice in 1512 have been well preserved. The Vodnjan mummies are kept in the church sanctuary behind the main altar. In addition to the parish church there are other smaller and larger sacral buildings in Vodnjan. Of special interest are the Baroque church of Our Carnelian Lady built from 1630-1664 and the church of St Mary Traversa which has an interesting relief altar pallas from the XVIIth century.

Gothic palace in Vodnjan

Vodnjan, Merchant street

Fažana

Fažana is situated on the coast 8 kilometers to the northwest of Pola and directly opposite the Brioni islands. It was settled as far back as Antiquity. At the beginning of the XXth century remnants of a large Roman villa rustica with richly decorated floor mosaics displaying floral and geometrical motifs was discovered in the nearby cove of Valbandon. A large ceramic workshop for making the most diverse types of amforas was situated alongside this rich and luxurious country house. The amforas served as containers for transporting different agricultural products of southern Istria such as wine, olive oil, grain and salted and marinated fish.

The church of St Eliseus from the VIth century, built on the ruins of a late Antique country castle erected in the earlier century, has been preserved in Fažana. The small church of St Mary of Carmel from the XIVth century with a built on portico safekeeps in its interior frescos from the XVth century.

The parish church of St Kuzma and Damjan is located on the coast itself and it bears Gothic features. Its sacristy keeps the remnants of Renaissance frescos from the XVIth century.

For a long time Fažana was important for its fishing but today it is turning more and more towards tourism.

Large Brioni island, air photo

The Brioni islands

The group of Brioni islands consists of two larger islands called Big and Small Brioni and 12 islets: Vanga, Jerolim, Kozada; Gaz, Vrsar, Galija, Madona, Okrugljak, Grunj, Supin, Supinić and St Mark. They are only 3 kilometers distant from the Istrian coast separated by the wide Fažana canal. The islands are situated almost at the very northwestern exit from the port of Pola.

The continuity of human habitation on these islands can be followed from prehistoric times. On the cape of Ploče on Big Brioni island remnants of a dugout settlement from the earlier Stone Age have been discovered. On the rises of Big Brioni island - on Kosir, Ciprovac, Antunovac, gradini and Straži - just as on the elevation of St Mikula on Little Brioni island there are ruins of Illyrian fort-hill settlements. After the Roman conquest of Istria life on Brioni islands was similar to that in the fertile space of southern Istria which was generally covered with large country houses with luxurious villas. Such architectural complexes have been found and presented on a number of locations. On the Big Brioni island they are located in the Bay of Veriga, the bay of Dobrika and on the elevations of Kolci and Gradina, in the St Mikula inlet on Small Brioni island and on the eastern side of the island of Vanga. The most sumptuous is without doubt the complex of the country castle in the bay of Veriga built in the Ist century after Christ. The excavated remains of this complex encompass a space of approximately five hectares. The section having to do with economic activity consists of the anchorage, a water pool, a fishery and a wool-mill while the sumptuous part of the castle consists of a complex of rooms for the landowner, guests and servants. The remnants of three temples have been preserved.

During late Antiquity the three-naved basilica of St Mary (probably the Vth century) was erected while the small church of St Peter dates from the early Byzantine period from the VIth century. During Byzantine rule a large, well fortified castrum was built in the bay of Dobrika where life went on up to the XVIth century.

In the XIth century a Benedictine monastery was erected alongside the Old Christian basilica of St Mary but was abandoned in 1312 because of the plague. It was restored in

89

Large Brioni island, remains of a sumptuous Roman summer house

the XVIth century and the basilica was in use up to the beginning of the XVIIIth century. A defence and residential tower with a rectangular ground plan - a donjon - was built in the XIIth or the beginning of the XIIIth century. In the XVIth century a citadel and another profane building was built alongside the existing donjon.

From 1331 the Brioni islands were ruled by Venice and this four centuries long period is characterised by a merciless exploitation of the Brioni forests and rocks. A larger settlement developed during the Venetian period on the eastern side of the islands.

Life on the Brioni islands totally ceased in the XVIIIth and the first half of the XIXth century. In addition to a number of plague epidemics the islands were at the mercy of malaria. During the construction and fortification of the harbour of Pola the Austrian monarchy built seven fortifications on the Brioni islands which were supposed to protect the sea approach into the bay. The largest was the "Tegetthof" fortification erected on the hill of Vela straža on Big Brioni island which at the time of its construction was the sturdiest fort on the Mediterranean.

Above:
Brioni, the remains of a large fortified building called
"the Byzantium castrum" in Dobrika bay on the western
side of Large Brioni island.

In 1893 the Brioni islands were bought by the Austrian industrialist Paul Kupelwieser who in the years before WWI had transformed the desolate islands into one of the most fashionable and attractive summer resorts. As a start he totally wiped out malaria with the aid of the renowned German physician and Nobel prize winner Robert Koch. He proceeded to clear away the maqui, put the woods and parks in order and planted different kinds of trees and bushes. The Brioni islands were settled by a number of species of small and large animals and a zoo was established. Simultaneously, large archeological excavations were organised and the findings were used to refine the natural beauty of the area. Exemplary vineyards and olive groves were organised in other sections of the islands. A new landing, a water supply system and an electrical plant, four luxury hotels and a number of individual villas in the style of the Art Nouveau movement were constructed on the tidied land. As early as the first decade of the twentieth century the Brioni summer resort had a closed pool with hot water. Amongst visitors to this exclusive destination were the crowned heads of Europe and many famous figures from high society. The Brioni summer resort went through a period of greatest prosperity in 1912

Air photo of the historical center of Pola, view from the southeast

and 1913. After WWI the resort remained a luxurious destination but the exclusivity of the guests never regained the
pre-war levels. During WWII the Allies bombed the Brioni
islands with destructive intensity so that they came out of the
war in a demolished state. In 1947 the islands became the
official summer residence of Josip Broz Tito and remained
so till his death in 1980. New luxury buildings were built
while the parks, glades and the Brioni woods were restored
and enriched. New species were added to the animal kingdom. Archeological excavations continued and the villas and
the parks were refined by works of contemporary sculpture.
All of these activities were done with a certain feeling for
measure so that the ecological balance was not undermined.
During this period the Brioni islands were visited by the
most eminent world politicians and certain historically significant meetings took place there. Since 1983 the Brioni
islands ahve been under protection and they now have the
status of a national park. Today the islands are moving in the
direction of exclusive tourism and are becoming a desirable
destination for excursions.

Pula

Pola is the dominant and largest city center on the Istrian peninsula. The city is situated at the head of a well-
indented and deep bay which, since its founding, has given
it the important role of being a good port and a secure
anchorage. The geographical position of Pola, located only
a bit to the west of the southernmost cape of the Istrian
peninsula, assigned the city in many historical periods a special strategic significance. This was particularly true of times
when the main routes along the Adriatic seacoast were
determined by the technology of sailing. The harbour -
owing to its dimensions and prominent position, the islets in
the harbour which divide the harbour space into a number
of basins and its excellent approach from the open sea and
the possibility of easily fortifying the coast - these are some
of the reasons why even today maritime scholarship holds
Pola harbour to be one of the best and the most secure natural ports in the world.

The position of the Pola amphitheatre in relation to the seacoast

The founding of the city as is often the case in the history of Mediterranean places, because of intermittent and complex migrations, contacts and intermingling of civilisations, is enveloped in legends. The most famous of these is the one that connects the founding of the city to the myth of the Argonauts and according to which the city was founded by the Greeks, refugees from Kolhida who made it to the Istrian coast. Verses by the famous Greek poet Kalimah refer to this event. The origin of this legend must surely be sought in the connections the Illyrian inhabitants of Istria successfully established with Greek sailors and the intensive trade with the Greeks, evinced by numerous archeological findings. The area around Pola was inhabited in the early Paleolithic age, proof of which are the findings from the nearby Šandalj cave. Settlements and fortifications from the Illyrian period were located on numerous sites in the environs of Pola while the city itself rose on an Illyrian hill-fort which was situated on the hill overlooking the bay (today this is the citadel). The name itself - Pola - is of Illyrian origins and designated some kind of hydrographic concept,

probably a water spring or perhaps the city as such. Illyrian Pola existed in the shadow of the more powerful Illyrian center Nesactium which was situated in its immediate vicinity and was the political, administrative, military and religious center of the whole region. The Roman conquest of the Istrian peninsula was of special significance to the development of Pola and its rapid urban expansion. After 177 BC the new Roman order was in force and Pola and its harbour served as a Roman bridgehead for further conquests of the neighbouring areas. In the second half of the Ist century BC it became a powerful military stronghold and finally an important trading emporium and harbour for the exchange of various goods. Around 43 BC Pola received the status of a colony. During the Civil war Pola first sided with Pompei and was subsequently severely destroyed by Ceaser's supporters. When the conflict continued after Ceaser's violent death Pola sided with his killers Brutus and Cassius so that it again suffered heavy damages at the hands of the military forces of the triumphant triumvir of Octavius, Anthony and Lepid. Because of the strategic and economic signif-

View of the amphitheatre from the southwest

Exhibition of Roman amphoras from the Ist-IVth century in the underground rooms of the amphitheatre

icance of the city, Octavius, now become the emperor Augustus, rebuilt Pola. His reign saw the building of some of the most beautiful Roman edifices. From that time and continuing throughout the entire Roman period of the emperors up to the Vth century Antique Pola experienced an unbroken development. During the time of the empire Pola was known as "Colonia Iulia Pola Pollentia Herculanea". Its ager, the agricultural land under its jurisdiction, spread all the way from the bay of Lim to the mouth of the river Raša on the sea. Very intensive economic activity developed in this area which secured for Pola wealth and significance. Agriculture, especially olive groves and vineyards were intensively tilled. This is testified to by numerous findings of large and wealthy countryside holdings, "villa rusticas". Fishing was highly developed on the seacoast and it supplied overseas markets with conserved products. From the area around Rovinj to

*The peripheral wall of the amphitheatre has two rows
with 72 vaults each and 64 square openings near its top*

*Underground quarters under the amphitheatre, the exhibition "Olive- nad
Wine-growing in Istria during Antiquity". A reconstruction of a wine-press*

the Brioni islands are to be found numerous Roman quarries which primarily served to supply building material to the city of Pola but also to other Roman towns and settlements in Istria. As mentioned earlier, a large pottery work existed in Fažana near Pola which produced amforas, vases and other kinds of pottery vessels which served as "containers"for the transportation of grain, oil, wine, conserved or salted fish and other products of the fertile south Istrian land. The city of Pola, especially from the time of Augustus, was built in accordance with the traditional Roman urban ideas. While the first Roman military camp - castrum - was situated on the hill on the site of the onetime Illyrian hill-fort (Citadel), the civilian urban buildings began to be constructed in an elliptical perimeter around the hill down to the seashore. The settlement was built according to a system of symmetrical city blocs - insulas. These formed a row of streets which

Double doors, Porta Gemina, the middle of the IInd century

spread out radially from the foot of the hill. Transversally they were connected by a number of concentric roads which followed the elliptical configuration of the central rise. On the slopes of Pola hill the Romans built a number of luxurious villas for prominent city families. The entire city space was encircled by defence walls whose foundations or parts have been well preserved on the eastern side of the city including three Roman city gates. Owing to the wealth garnered by the import-export harbour, the Roman city houses were richly furnished and decorated with mosaics. Some extraordinary examples such as the one containing the mythological scene of the Punishment of Dirce have been preserved. The forum with its attendant buildings and temples and a propylaea leading from the forum to the citadel stood on the western part of the city, almost on the very edge of the sea. Roman Pola had two theatres. The smaller one was located within the city walls while the much larger one was built to the south of the city. To the northeast in the immediate vicinity of the city center at the foot of the hill Kaštanjer, alongside the main road of the time which lead to Aquileia, a larger amphitheater was built in the Ist cen-

tury. It could receive more than 20.000 spectators and is today the sixth according to size to be preserved worldwide. Gladiatorial combats and other widespread kinds of Roman entertainment for the masses were held in its arena. The size of the amphitheater and the large theatre located outside the city walls testify not only to the importance of Roman Pola (at the time it had a little over 5.000 inhabitants) but to the relative density of population in southern Istria for the entertainment of whose populace these large constructions were erected.

Christian places of worship sprang up in Roman Pola as early as the IVth century. The cathedral of St Mary in Pola was built in the Vth century on the foundations of the earlier church of St Thomas built a century earlier.

The migrations of peoples, the invasions by barbarian tribes and their inroads into the territory of the Roman empire were not reflected on the life of Pola because these large European movements, the battlelines and the frequent wars took place more to the north. This was particularly true of the attempt to penetrate the Italic peninsula. Due to this factor Pola remained an important Roman har-

Air photo of the remains of the small Roman theatre on the slope under the Citadel

bour up to the end of the Vth century. Near the end of the Vth century, after the fall of the western Roman Empire, Pola was briefly under the rule of the eastern Goths. During the thirties of the VIth century the Byzantine emperor Justine undertook a large military campaign against the Goths in order to liberate the western regions. Justine's famous military leader Belizar with a numerous army disembarked in Pola in 544. The city together with the entire territory of Istria came under Byzantine rule and this lasted for more than two centuries (to 770). Pola, like the rest of Istria, was administratively joined to the Ravena exarchate. During the period of Byzantine rule Pola maintained important trading connections with the eastern Mediterranean. The large basilica of St Mary Formosa, a masterpiece of early Byzantine art, was built at the time in Pola. Incursions by the Slavs and the gradual settlement of Istria got under way during the second half of the VIth century. Flights of the earlier inhabitants, the abandonment of production and the gradual but fundamental destruction of the remnants of the Antique world were some of the consequences.

Following a fate common to the entire region, near the end of the VIIIth century Pola fell under the power of the Franks. The new feudal relations and interests enabled in large measure the settling down of the Slavic, predominantly Croatian, farmers on the devastated Istrian lands. On the other hand, the new relationships fueled resistance and contributed to the self-consciousness of the older coastal communities and Pola was amongst these. During the Middle Ages Pola was under the influence of the two dominant powers in the north Adriatic area - the power of the Aquileian patriarch which was on the wane and the growing domination of the new power of the Venetian Republic. Vacillating between these two powers Pola, together with other Istrian towns, made an alliance with Venice relatively early (at the beginning of the XIth century). Already by the end of the XIth century the navy of Pola was big enough to participate in the transportation of Crusaders to the east during the First Crusade campaign. With its growing strength on the sea Pola would at times endanger Venetian interests and attack its ships so that the Venetian navy had to engage in war campaigns against it. Frequent conflicts of interests on the north Adriatic led to numerous seabattles between the navies of the Mediterranean maritime states. In such a manner from the XIIth to the XIVth century Pola underwent attacks by Pizana and Genova forces. Coming under the rule of Venice in 1331 Pola was attacked and

Temple of Augustus on the Pola forum

A Roman temple probably dedicated to the goddess Diana has been built into the rear part of the Medieval City Hall

overrun a number of times by Genova forces. Especially destructive was the defeat of the Venetian fleet in front of Pola in 1379. On this occassion the Genovese overtook and plundered and ransacked the city to such an extent that Medieval Pola never recovered. Its trading significance was destroyed and most of its inhabitants fled. Epidemics of the plague harassed the region especially in the XVth century while the nearby deserted marshes brought the permanent threat of malaria. The city was demolished and the famous Pola antique architecture lay in ruins. In spite of its devastated condition the architecture of Pola was the cause of admiration amongst many renowned sculptors and builders. Famous Renaissance artists such as Sangalla, Sansovina, Michelangelo and Palladia immortalized Pola with their sketches and drawings. According to eyewitness reports hardly 300 people lived in Pola in the XVIIth century. Because the city, even in such a calamatious state was,

because of its harbour and anchorage, the target of attacks by forces from Senj (Uskoci), the Venetian Republic decided to build new fortifications. A new fortress was built and the neglected harbour put in order during the first half of the XVIIth century. In connection with this it ought to be noted that despite the decline of the city the harbour of Pola throughout the period of Venetian rule continued to be an important station on the route to the Levant and back. Ships of many Mediterranean shipping and merchant countries found anchorage in the harbour. After the fall of Venice and by the treaty in Campoformio in 1797 Pola was turned over to the Austrian monarchy under whose rule it remained, with a short interval of French Napoleonic rule (1805-1814), up to the demise of the monarchy during WWI in 1918. Because of the new political and economic conditions during the first half century of Austrian rule Pola lost its importance as a harbour and the city continued to

The City hall and Augustus's temple on the site of the onetime Roman forum

decline. The events which wholly changed the course of development of the city were played out on the Italian peninsula. The struggle of the Italian people for unification, supported as it was by the European powers, totally endangered Austrian possessions on Italian territory so that the Monarchy had to seek a more secure location for its main wartime harbour and naval arsenal than the one it had maintained in Venice. The choice of the emperor's commission fell on Pola. In 1856 a large naval arsenal for the building, equipment and repairment of the Austrian war fleet began to be built in the harbour of Pola. From that point the city began to rapidly develop, especially after 1866 when Pola received the status of the main base of the Austrian monarchy's war navy. Already during the construction of the arsenal the number of inhabitants had risen to 2.000 while during the middle of the eighties Pola numbered more than 20.000 inhabitants. Before WWI Pola had nearly 60.000 inhabitants of which more than ten thousands of employees worked in the arsenal itself and in its auxiliary workshops. The merchant part of the Pola harbour also came to life so that Pola registered a continual advancement as far as the economy was concerned. The life of the main

fleet base of the monarchy, encompassing as it did a nationally variegated population, was reflected in the composition of the new population in which representatives from all the peoples of the Austro-Hungarian monarchy were to be found. Notwithstanding the emphatic cosmopolitism of Austrian Pola (the Irish writer James Joyce was amongst the numerous foreigners who spent some time in Pola) it has to be underlined that in search of employment a large number of impoverished Istrian Croatian village people found themselves in the arsenal. The new requirements dictated by the military harbour, the arsenal and the numerous central military-maritime institutions totally transformed the appearance of the harbour and the city. The whole space of the harbour was secured by new fortifications and breakwaters. Large shipyard slipways and dry-docks were built on the islet of Uljanik in the middle of the harbour while floating docks and numerous plants and facilities of the arsenal and the naval station dotted the shore. Representative buildings were built in the city for the needs of the military command and numerous barracks and other military objects within the confines of the harbour. An entire new Pola was constructed to meet the needs of the arsenal work-

Pola, the Sergievian triumphal arch (Ist century BC) and markers of the position of the one time Roman Golden doors which were flanked by two circularly designed towers

ers, naval officers, technical engineers and state officials while the highest-ranking officers were given new villas and residences. Such expansive construction moved the perimeters of the city so that the Roman buildings such as the amphitheater, at one time outside of the city, found themselves in its very center.

After the dissolution of the Monarchy in 1918 Pola was occupied by Italian troops. After the Rapallo agreement in 1920 and thanks to the London agreement whereby the Allies persuaded the Kingdom of Italy to enter the war on their side after territorial concessions on the eastern Adriatic coast, Pola, together with the whole of Istria, was annexed to the Kingdom of Italy.

During the changed circumstances of Italian rule the strategic position of Pola harbour lost its onetime significance. Most of the earlier, particularly Croatian population, emigrated and Pola became only an administrative center showing tendencies of economic decline. Neither was the Italian population that remained spared the cruelties of the newly-established Fascist regime. During WWII Pola was affected by the whirlpool of war. After Italy capitulated it was occupied by German forces and underwent heavy bombardment. After the liberation in May 1945 it became a part of the Allied occupational zone A under Anglo-American administration. It was only after many diplomatic maneuvers and protests that it became in 1947 a part of Croatia within Federal Yugoslavia. The discontent caused by this decision amongst the Italian population was expressed in a new and painful exodus of the population of Pola similar to the one in 1918 but this time in the opposite direction. Although burdened by the huge presence of the Yugoslav army Pola began to develop and rebuild. Manufacturing industries developed alongside the traditional shipbuilding industry. However, tourism became more and more important for Pola owing to its attractive surroundings with numerous picturesque inlets. Numerous complexes of hotels, tourist settlements and marinas were built on the periphery of the city and on locations nearby Pola. With this new and clear orientation Pola entered the new period of Croatian state independence after 1991.

What makes Pola an exceptionally interesting destination and gives it a specific significance on the artistic and touristic map of this part of Europe are, first of all, its excellent architectonic and artistic monuments from the Antique and Medieval period.

The most monumental is doubtlessly the large Roman amphitheater know as the Arena in popular jargon. Because of its dimensions it was built beyond the city walls. Its construction leans upon and incorporates one of the slopes of Kaštanjer hill. In Roman times it was situated on what was then the main road, Via Flavia, which led towards Aquileia. The first, somewhat smaller amphitheater was built on the same site by the emperor Augustus at the beginning of the Ist century as part of the large reconstruction of Pola. The building was expanded in the middle of the Ist century during the reign of Claudious and received its final shape around the eighties of the Ist century during the time of emperor Vespasianus. The Pola amphitheater was completed at the same time as the famous Colosseum in Rome. As mentioned, it is the sixth largest preserved object of its kind in the world. Its ground is elliptical in shape. Its longer axis is almost 133 meters long while the shorter one is 105 meters in length. The central section of the amphitheater, the arena, where the gladiatorial combats were staged, is 67,90 x 41,60 meters in size. The interior of the amphitheater, the auditorium with stone benches and parts of the supporting construction, has not been preserved because the abandoned building through the centuries served as a kind of quarry from which materials were taken for the erection of the churches and other buildings in Pola. The monumental stone exterior of the amphitheater, which is rhythmically divided with two storeys of identical arcades with all together 72 vaults in each row and a topmost third storey with its 64 rectangular openings, has been preserved. Vertical grooves in which wooden masts were placed during summer events to support the awning roof of the amphitheater - the velarium - are visible on the inner side of this wall. A specific feature of the Pola amphitheatre are the four stone towers leaning on the outer side of the wall of the edifice. Their system of wooden stairways facilitated the entrance into the auditorium and the emptying of the amphitheatre at the end of the performance. During the time it was fully functional the amphitheatre had about twenty entrances for spectators. Underground rooms with apparatuses for raising the gladiators, spaces for animals and other equipment used in specific performances were situated immediately underneath the arena. Today in these underground chambers of the Arena one can visit the per-

Pola, the orthodox church of St Nicholas built in the VIth century

The vault of the southern chapel of the basilica of St Mary Formosa

manent exhibition "Olive Growing and Wine-Growing in Istria during Antiquity" which beside various reconstructed antique agricultural equipment - mills, presses and such - offers to the viewer a large collection of the most various kinds and shapes of amphoras which were used to transport wine and oil.

Different cultural events are nowadays staged in the Arena. The auditorium can accept 5.000 spectators while the stone surrounding wall offers an excellent setting for various musical performances, concerts and opera stagings. The Arena is the place where the Festival of Croatian Film is traditionally held.

The Roman forum, the central antique square, was built on the western side of the city immediately next to the sea so that land had to be reclaimed before its construction got under way. This is a rectangular space 37 x 81 meters in size around which were located the most important buildings of the religious, administrative and judiciary life of the city as well as places of economic activity such as the market and numerous shops. Three temples stood on the north side of the capitol. The oldest stood in the middle and was consecrated to the so-called capitol triad - Jupiter, Juno and Minerva. A temple devoted to his Highness the emperor and the goddess Roma was erected to the right during the reign of emperor Augustus. During the reign of emperor Vespazia, the city basilica to the left of the central temple was demolished and the so-called Diana temple was built whose

dimensions and form harmonised with the already erected temple to Augustus. A porch decorated with colonnades and sculptures which led into various public rooms encompassed the remaining three sides of forum. During the Middle Ages the forum retained its role of being the central communal square but some tearing down and alternations took place during which the greater part of Antique architecture disappeared and a new communal palace was built - the city hall. The stone pavement of the Roman forum which lies 120 centimeters under the present surface of the square has been preserved intact. Augustus's temple has been wholly preserved while the back wall of Diana's temple was used in the construction of the municipal palace and is clearly visible at its rear. Other fragments of Roman architecture can be found only in portions of walls or during archeological excavations of the surrounding space.

Augustus's temple is a handsome and well-proportioned building which, although not having large dimensions, gives the impression of monumentality. It was erected during the reign of Augustus (2 BC - 14 AD). Its base is rectangular and forms a high pedestal. The rear of the temple consists of a closed cella. An open pronaos whose facade contains four columns while its wings have each one column forms the front of the temple. The columns are smooth with richly decorated Corinthian capitals while the corner pilasters of the cella have flutes on them. Under the roof a decorative relief frieze spans the entire length of the temple except

Pola, the preserved southern chapel of the basilica of St Mary Formosa (VIth century)

on the facade where at one time stood an inscription in bronze letters. The sculptures in the triangular gable of the facade have not been preserved.

After the Antique era the temple at one point served as a church and afterwards as a storage for grain. At the beginning of the XIXth century the Napoleonic marshal

The facade and the belfry of the cathedral of the Ascension of the Blessed Virgin Mary in Pola

Marmont launched an initiative to establish a collection of Antique stone monuments in the temple. During WWII it was hit by an airplane bomb and was almost totally destroyed. It was restored between 1945-1947. Today it houses the collection "Roman Portrait Sculpture".

During the Middle Ages the City Hall was built on the site of the other two temples. The greater part of its present appearance it owes to the thorough alterations done in 1296. The palace underwent numerous alternations, its facade was renovated in the XVIth century and again in the XVIIth century. During the time Pola was a free municipality the hall was a symbol of communal autonomy while it afterwards served as the seat of the Venetian administrator. From the XIXth century to our days it has been the headquarters of the city mayor. The eastern part of the building has partially preserved some features of late Romanesque art with its blind arches under the onetime lower roof cornice and corner sculptures of a crouching telamon and a siren. The southern, main facade has a ground floor portico with Renaissance columns.

Parts of the Roman fortification architecture and three preserved gates of the ten that the city once had are visible on the eastern foundations of the city. The most attractive was the gate which on its inner side had a lean-to very handsome triumphal arch of harmonious proportions. The woman patrician Salvia Postuma from the Sergio family had it made in honor of three members of her family who held high offices. One of them was Lucio Sergio Lepid, commander of the legion which participated on the side of Octavius Augustus in the battle near Akcia in 31 BC when Ceaser's murderers were defeated. The triumphal arch was erected not long after this event and signified victory. The simple, well-proportioned arch whose pilasters are divided on each side by two thin grooved Corinthian half columns is richly adorned with relief decorations. Under a strong and decorated cornice runs a frieze with reliefs depicting

Right:
Pola, the interior of the cathedral of the Ascension of the Blessed Virgin Mary. The epitaph of bishop Orsini on the floor

Apse and belfry of the Francsican church

Monumental portal of the monastery church of St Francis
Right: Pola, the interior of the monastey church of St Francis

weaponry. Vertical parts of the arch are decorated with relief motifs of vine grapes while its vault is cassetted. Its center depicts a scene of an eagle fighting a snake. Relief depictions of two flying Victorias - goddesses of victory - stand between the inner half-columns near the top of the vault. Above the cornice are stone pedestals for the figures of the three Sergias with inscriptions. Their sculptures have not been preserved. The Sergievian triumphal arch was conceived in such a manner to be viewed only from the inner side of the city gates ("Porta aurea"). Because of this its eastern side is much more modest in execution and lacks decorations. Since the walls and the gate itself were torn down during the process of urbanising the city in the XIXth century the triumphal arch is today a self-standing edifice.

Protected by two considerably older, probably Medieval halfcylindrical towers, the so-called gate of Hercules appears an extremely modest edifice. This is a vault opening

made of simply cut stone blocs which on its crown displays Hercules's roughly-chiselled bearded, curly-haired head. Hercules's club has been chiselled to the right in shallow relief. Next to the club is an inscription bearing the names of two Roman officials who were sent in the middle of the Ist century BC by the Roman state at the head of the settlers with the aim of establishing a colony in the bay of Pola.

The so-called Twin Gates (Porta Gemina), built at the turn of the IInd and IIIrd century, make two identical vault openings through which one entered into some kind of inner yard and only afterwards into the city itself. They are decorated with half-columns and half-capitals and the vaults of the arches show slots which loweverd the grating closing the passageway. During Roman times a necropolis was located in front of the Twin Gates with numerous sarcophaguses and tombstones of which the majority were used in Medieval times as building material. The octogonal

*The Venetian fortress the Citadel which dominates the high ground in the center of the city.
Today it houses the Historical Museum of Istria*

foundations of a Roman mausoleum have been preserved in the immediate vicinity of the gates.

In Roman times the Twin Gates led to the city theatre whose step-like auditorium used the slope of the city hill. Parts of the stage building and of the auditorium have been preserved. Another much larger theatre was located, like the amphitheater, outside the city walls and used the slope of the nearby hill Zaro. No significant fragment of this large edifice can today be seen. Its appearance is partially known to us because of old engravings of Pola. The facade of the large theatre was almost 100 meters long while the orchestar had a 25 meters radius. The auditorium had two storeys and its architectonics were richly modulated.

Of the numerous early Christian buildings that existed in Pola the architecture of the cathedral of the Assumption of the Blessed Virgin has in large part been preserved. Built on the site of the earliest sacral edifices (IVth century) today's building originated in the Vth century. It is a three-naved basilica whose raised sanctuary is separated from the space of the congregation by three arches. The bishop's lectern and the bench for the priests stood on the semicir-cular podium. The church underwent significant reconstructions after the fire of 1242 and again in the XVth century. Thusly the windows of the aisles have Gothic window openings. The wing portal of the cathedral from 1457 is decorated with Renaissance reliefs and was taken from the torn down Benedictine abbey of St Michael on Vrh. The cathedral facade was renovated in 1712 in the spirit of early Venetian Classicism. The self-standing belfry was completed the same year in 1707. The cathedral baptistry from the end of the Vth century, which used to stand in front of it, was torn down in 1885. At one time the very old church of St Thomas, raised at the turn of the IVth and the Vth century and torn down in the Middle Ages, used to stand in the park alongside the south side of the Pola cathedral.

During Byzantine rule in the Vth century the large three-naved basilica of St Mary Formosa was erected. It had two wing sepulchral chapels with a circular ground plan. The complex was torn down in the XVIth century and only the southern chapel has been preserved. Today's Orthodox church of St Nicholas, a one-naved building which underwent reconstruction at the end of the XIIth century, dates

Pola, the neoclassical building of the one time Austrian Admirality from 1861

back to the same period. A valuable iconostas from the XVIIIth century, the work of the Greek master Tomios Batosa, can be found in the church.

The monastery and church of St Francis are situated on the slope of the hill between the forum and the citadel. The Franciscans were to be found in Pola as far back as the XIIIth century and their large monastrery church was completed in 1314. This is a monumental one-naved church for holding sermons with three square apses covered by cross-corrugated vaults which open towards the space of the church with Gothically sharp triumphal arches. The facade of the church has a monumental and richly decorated portal. A high quality wooden polyptych with two rows of poly-chromonised depictions of saints in relief and with a richly carved frame are to be found on the main altar in the church. The work was probably made during the middle of the XVth century. Three wings of the monastery are conjoined to the church forming a rectangular cloister. It was erected at the same time as the church but was reconstructed in the XVth century. The columns of the cloister show early Renaissance features. The chapel of St John, later

transformed into a capitular hall and decorated with sumptuous Gothic biforia, is located in the middle of the east wing. A collection of Medieval stone statues, the property of the Archeological Museum of Istria, are exhibited in the monastery cloister.

The large bastion fortress on the Citadel is the most significant and the oldest edifice as far as fortification architecture of the newer period is concerned. It stands on the high ground overlooking the city, on the strategically most prominent place where the main city fortifications had been built before it for millenniums. The fortress was built as it now stands by the Venetian Republic in 1630 according to plans made by the French military architect Antoin De Ville. It is a fortress with a very regular ground plan. The core consists of a large square of powerful walls from whose corners spread out in a star like fashion pointed pentagonal bastions. As the significance of Pola harbour was very great for safe sailing on the main maritime route to the East this fortress with its bastions and artillery had to safeguard the harbour and the city. Today it houses the Historical Museum of Istria which has in its possession a large number of

Pola, the naval church of Our Lady of the Sea (1891-1898)

sive construction from the middle of the XIXth century up to 1914, have been preserved despite the heavy air bombardments during WWII. The following buildings merit special mention: the very harmonious neo-Classicist building of the admirality built in 1861 on the waterfront, the representative and luxurious hotel "Riviera" from 1908 which, despite a mixture of styles, shows the dominant mode of the Wien Secession, the richly decorated Secession building of the Boarding school for girls from 1907 (today's Pedagogical faculty) and the navy church of Our Lady of the Sea (1891-1898) built in a mixture of neo-Romanesque and neo-Byzantine styles.

The Market building erected in 1903 according to plans by the engineer L. Nobis is a special architectural attraction in Pola. This large two-storeyed building was built as a steel construction with glass. Stone was only used for the stairway in front of the wing facades and for the main entrance. The Market building conjoins the modern use of new construction material and an emphatic Secessionist aesthetic.

The Archeological Museum of Istria, one of the most important of its kind in Croatia, is located in the onetime Royal secondary school building from 1890. It was founded in 1902. It exhibits the material culture of the Istrian peninsula and of the islands of Cres and Lošinj from prehistory to the early Middle Ages. The collected exhibits are the result of numerous and thorough archeological excavation that have been carried out on numerous Istrian localities in the XIXth and the XXth century. It has a particularly valuable collection of Antique and early Medieval sculpture.

objects and the most various museum pieces that bear witness to the historical developments of the Istrian peninsula. Various cultural events are staged in the central yard of the fortress.

Under Austrian rule and fulfilling the new role that was assigned to Pola an almost new city was built with the pronounced influence of Middle European architectural taste and culture. This encompassed theatres, large public buildings, museums, schools, hotels, residential quarters with villas as well as tramcars and electric lights. Quite a number of buildings endowed with a stylistic excellence or undoubtable environmental value, dating to the period of inten-

Vizače (Nesactium)

About 11 kilometers to the east of Pola on a high ground near the village of Valtura is Vizače one of the most significant archeological localities in Istria. Because of such a dominant position, a very important prehistorical settlement, which in the Illyrian period became the

main political and religious center of the Illyrian tribe Histri, developed on this locality. In antiquity Vizača was called Nesactium. Extensive archeological research that got under way around 1900 and continued several times during

Vizače (Nesactium), remains of the city walls, Roman edifices and the complex of the Early Christian churches

Mutvoran, City Gate

Illyrian cult building. A spacious square forum with a porch was built to the east of the capitol. The Roman settlement with its public baths and other public buildings, workshops, markets and residential quarters which sloped downhill spread around this complex. The city had three large tanks for water and a sewage system.

From the IVth century Nesactium became more and more a fortified late Antique citadel. It was given walls, a defence tower and a number of gates. During the construction of these the earlier buildings were torn down and a large part of them, especially those outside the walls, were abandoned. The early Christian period was characterised by the finding of a twin basilica of the Aquileian type constructed in the Vth century. The two buildings were connected by a common narthex.

Nesactium was destroyed during the Slav-Avarian forays into Istria between 599-611 and was never restored. Today it is a well ordered archeological locality with a smaller building, the property of the Istrian Archeological Museum, in which are presented the phases of archeological excavations and the buildings and urban texture of the Antique settlement interpreted through ground maps.

Mutvoran

To the east of the Labin-Pola road nearby Marčane sits the small village of Mutvoran under the remains of whose Medieval fortifications are hidden the cyclopean walls of one of the mysterious Illyrian cities, probably Faveria. The Medieval walls have been integrated into the later residential houses. Ruins of the tower and the entrance gate have been preserved. The parish church of St Mary Magdalen was built in the XIIIth century in the Romanesque manner. The church belongs to the state-room type with three inscribed apses covered by barrel-like vaults. The facade of the church exibits Renaissance traits. A number of houses with Renaissance facades have been preserved in Mutvoran.

the XXth century discovered within the fort-hill settlement a large Histrian necropolis of cremated burial remains with numerous ceramic urns and rich burial offerings of imported painted vessels.

The necropolis has been dated to the time from the XIth to the IVth century BC. These important findings are exhibited in the Istrian Archeological Museum in Pola.

Roman troops overran Nesactium after the decisive victory over the Histrians under the walls of the settlement in 1777 BC. A Roman settlement, a municipium, began developing on this site and numerous conserved remnants of its architecture are visible today. A capitol with three temples built in the IInd century merits special attention. A larger, central temple stands in the middle and a smaller one on each side. The complex of temples was partially built on the site of the earlier

Barban

Barban is situated to the northeast of Pola on the road to Labin near the mouth of the river Raša. It was a Medieval fortified settlement belonging to the Pazin duchy and from the XVIth century it came under the rule of Venice. The Venetian government sold it at an auction in 1535 to the Loredan family. In the middle of the settlement stood a citadel whose northern part was adopted at the beginning of the XVIIIth century into the large one-naved parish church of St Nicholes. The church belfry was built upon the Medieval tower. The Loredan palace was built in 1606 through the adaptation of the eastern part of the citadel. It stands out with its Baroque facade and in the rear with a spacious porch on the first floor. Two gates from the XVIIIth century have been preserved. The Big Gate leads to the town square while the Small Gate opens up to the street on which stand the county hall and the clock tower

Barban, the parish church of St Nicholas, the view through the porch of the Loredan palace

from the XVIth century. Of interest is the small congregationist church of St Anthony the Monk in front of the Big Gate in which remnants of Gothic frescos from the XVth century are kept.

Recently Barban has renewed the traditional chivalry game "The race of the Ring" which has a tradition going back to 1696. The competition consists of horsemen at a gallop competing to hit with their lance a double metal ring. The game is very similar to the famous Alka games in Sinj and attracts many visitors to Barban.

Barban, porch and yard of the Loredan palace (XVIIth century)

Old and new Labin

Labin

Labin is a typical Istrian town of the acropolis type that was built on an Illyrian hill-fort. During Roman times it was the castrum Albona while in the early Middle Ages it was one of the first Istrian towns to assume a Croatian identity. For a long period of time it was under the rule of the Aquileian patriarchs and from 1420 it came under the rule of the Venetian Republic.

In the beginning the Medieval fortified town occupied only the top of the hill (so-called Gorica) around the parish church. Since the town, because of its strategic importance, expanded in the XVIth century it was given a new ring of walls which encompassed the slopes of the hill (Dolica). In newer times the miner's settlement Podlabin which by the middle of the XXth century had the marks of

an urban enviroment formed at the foot of the old town of Labin.

The monumental main city gate of St Florus was built during the construction of the outer rings of fortification. The inner part of the gate dates back to 1437 while the out-

er representative entrance was completed in 1346. The sides are composed of wide, tumescent stone parallelepipeds which rhythmically follow in succession smaller, indented, regularly cut parallelepipeds. A rectangular attic with an inscription, flanked by two cartouches displaying coats of

arms stands above the gate. The gate ends with a triangular gable in which stands the image of the Venetian lion. By its features this monument is close to the Mannirist taste of the end of the XVIth century but its emphatic plasticity anticipates the spirit of the early Baroque.

The new city square Črč, with an irregular ground plan and on slanting terrain, was formed outside the walls. A Baroque municipal loggia stands out on this square. This building from 1662 (restored in 1777) is held to be the most handsome example of baroque architecture in buildings of this kind in Istria. It was conceived as a spacious porch with stone benches opened on three sides. The wooden roof rests upon thin columns. A collection of stone monuments from Antiquity to the period of the Venetians is today housed in the loggia.

Owing to its location on hilly terrain the urban texture of Labin is huddled, full of elevations and stairways and the houses and the streets conform to the configuration of the terrain. Tall buildings with three or more storeys dominate the town. Labin abounds in handsome examples of patrician palaces from the Renaissance and Baroque period. The edifices that stand out are the Renaissance palace Scampicchio from the XVth century with its inner yard, the Baroque palace Franković-Vlačić, Manzin, Negri from the XVIIth century and the representative palace Battiala-Lazzaribi from the first half of the XVIIIth century.

The Battiala-Lazzarini palace is one of the best preserved authentic Baroque palaces in Istria. The ground floor facade is characterised by a robust and monumental stone portal whose door-posts were built according to a scheme of rhythmically alternating a larger after two smaller stone parallelepipeds. Over the door the stone parallelepipeds broaden out in a fan-like fashion to form a vault. The key stone always has the form of a robust volute. The frames of the two window openings flanking the portal almost grew into it. The portal leads into the ground floor atrium of the building, some kind of room for doing business. The inner portal from which the stairway leads to the first floor is almost equally monumental. On the first floor over the atrium is a large hall, a salon whose three large Baroque window openings with semicircular vaults open onto the street (so called "piano nobile"). The openings stand closely together so that as much light as possible enter the representative hall. The lower parts of the windows are protected by stone para-

Labin, the city gate of St Florus (XVIIth century)

Labin, the facade of the Baroque chapel of St Stephen

pets with close-built balusters in the shape of a double pear. The keystones of the window vaults end in robustly modulated marble human heads. The same arrangement is repeated on the second floor so that the Lazzarini palace belongs amongst the more sumptuous Istrian secular buildings on which the "piano nobile" makes a double appearance. The facade ends with a third storey and its wholly simple square windows. Through the emphatic and somewhat robust plasticity of its facade the Lazzarini palace stands out from the surrounding space in spite of the large stone volume of the parish church in its immediate vicinity. Of the public buildings mention ought to be made of the Pretorian palace with its Renaissance biforia and the city storage house for grain completed in 1539. As the storage place lost its function in the XIXth century it was reconstructed into the theatre building in 1843. The clock tower located immediately next to the storage was built in the middle of the XVIIth century.

The spacious parish church of the Deliverance of the Blessed Virgin Mary was built in the XIVth century in the Gothic style with a large rosette on its facade. The building underwent thorough reconstruction in the XVIth century. The alternation of its interior was completed at the beginning of the XVIIth century. A very interesting Baroque bust of the senator and soldier Antonio Bollania was built into its facade in 1688. The youngish, masculine and dignified face of the senator is enframed by thick curly hair and the drapery of his mantle contrasts with the stiffness of the metal armor. The bust is placed between flags and trophies and presents the Baroque concept of sculpture in the best possible manner. Going by its plastic quality it is one of the most handsome examples of secular baroque sculpture in Istria.

Interior of the parish church of Blessed Mary in Childbirth in Labin

The smaller chapel of St Stephen on a small slanting square from the XVIIIth century connects the space between the parish church and the large Battiala-Lazzarini palace. Its facade with two large, Baroquely profiled window openings and doors over which stand characteristic Baroque eaves is one of the most handsome and most Baroque facades amongst the small Istrian churches.

The church belfry built in 1623 is a self-standing edifice somewhat distanced from the parish church and is located at the very top of the hill.

On the access road under Labin stands the smaller church of St Mary of Health which has an interesting Baroque porch with very thin columns which enable the Baroque facade with the portal and two very low rectangular windows on the sides to be easily seen.

A large country house built in the XVIIth century of the onetime powerful Labin family Franković-Vlačić stands in Dubrova in the immediate vicinity of Labin. Its spatial arrangement, disposition and architectural appearance can even today conjure, although fragmentarily, the quality of country living of the rich Istrian noblemen.

Large underground coalmines, that reach underneath the old city itself, are located in the immediate vicinity of Labin. The old historical center was endangered by the possible caving in of the earth. The mining of coal was brought to a halt in 1972 and the subsiding of the earth was stopped which enabled the restoration and the revitalisation of the old city center.

The Labin Folk museum with its archeological, ethnographic and cultural-historical collections and its gallery of art works is now housed in the Battiala-Lazzarini palace. Numerous ateliers for artists have been furbished in Labin while an International symposium for sculptors is active in Dubrova. The artistic manifestation "The New Artistic Meetings in Labin" has been organised since 1993.

Old Plomin

Plomin

The old town of Plomin is situated above the relatively deep and narrow bay of Plomin which was created while the river Boljunčica flowed into the sea at that location. Today its water disappears into the nearby Čepić-Polje.

Plomin is a very old town. Antiquity mentions it as Flanona and the gulf of Kvarner got its name from it in Antiquity - Sinus Flanaticus.

Like many other Istrian towns it began its existence as an Illyrian hill-fort while in Roman times it was an important harbour and municipium. During the Middle Ages it was a fortified town. A number of Renaissance and Baroque houses stand out within the huddled urban texture. The church of St George the Elder is a one-naved Romanesque building. Romanesque biforia are visible on its south wall. A characteristic Romanesque belfry was added to its western side. The church was expanded on its eastern side in the XVIth century. The parish church of St George is a Late Gothic building completed in 1474 and built upon during the Baroque period.

Nowadays old Plomin is almost deserted and this has contributed to its further decline.

Mošćenice and the Mošćenička Draga

The massif of the Učka mountain overlooks eastern Istria and falls steeply toward the seacoast. Settlements are rare and it is only quite recently that they come to the shore. The eastern coast of Istria from the gulf of Plomin to the gulf of Prelučki has been traditionally called the Liburnia coastline relying thusly on the old historical designation for the space from Raša towards the east which was at one time settled by the Liburian tribe. The southern part of the Liburnian coast is steep, lacking protected inlets so that the settlements were formed on the high grounds, generally in

The old town Mošćenice

places where the old roads could follow the configuration of the terrain.

The southernmost of these is Brseč, situated on a rock 150 meters above the sea. Because of the importance of its location it became a fortification in the VIth century and in the Middle Ages the settlement formed around the citadel. In time the onetime fortifications intertwined with the outer row of houses. Brseć offers a magnificent view of the gulf of Kvarner and the neighbouring islands.

Mošćenice, somewhat to the north, a Medieval fortified town situated 173 meters over the sea, is similarly situated. The settlement is very closely packed and compact, huddled near the very top of a hill. The three-naved parish church of St Andrew and its massive belfry dominate the steeps. Originally the church was a one-naved space which at the beginning of the XVIIIth century first got a sanctuary and was then at the end of the same century extended with side aisles. St Andrew was completed with the quiet dignified forms of Baroque Classicism and reminds the viewer of a Middle European city church. Its belfry was given a cupola in 1658. Some smaller churches are also interesting: St Sebastian from 1501 and St Bartholomew from 1628, both with the characteristic Istrian porch - "lopica".

Of the secular buildings what has been preserved is the town gate from 1642, defended by a tower standing on a rectangular ground plan. The municipal loggia stands in front of the gate. The outer walls of the peripheral row of houses were built in such a manner as to replace the city walls. The Negovetić-Dešković house and the Negotević palace from 1770 stand out with their representative facades.

Streams and intermittent torrents falling down the mountain formed a small cove immediately underneath Mošćenica where a small and picturesque fishing village Mošćenička Draga came into being. Since the whole bay has a pebbly beach the place has become a very attractive tourist settlement which attracts numerous tourists during the summer months.

Lovran

Where the Učka steeps fall a bit more gently towards the sea a narrow strip of seashore was created which enabled the building of settlements. When tourism began in the XXth century it was here that winter and summer tourism for the rich clients of the Austrian empire began to develop. In time the region became one of the best known tourist destinations in the monarchy so that the building of hotels, sanatoriums and fashionable villas spread from Opatija to Lovran, creating the renowned Opatija riviera. In the period after WWII the international popularity of this destination enabled an even more intensive development of tourism which spread to the onetime smaller fishing settlements such as Ika and Ičići between Lovran and Opatija. This region is today one of the most significant tourist locations in Croatia especially because the mild climate, the beauty of the landscape, the numerous resorts, the sumptuous and comfortable architecture of the hotels, the well-ordered parks and long promenades along the sea and all the other urban felicities enable the tourist season to last the whole year round.

Lovran is the southernmost and the oldest town in this area. It is mentioned already in the VIIth century as Lauriana and the Arab geographer El Edrisi writes of it in 1153 as an important maritime and trade center. In the Middle Ages it is a Croatian community and later in the XVth century it came under the rule of the Pazin duchy.

Parts of the medieval fortifications have been preserved in the peripheral walls of the southern bloc of houses as well as the town gate, the so-called Stubica which leads to the sea. Many examples of picturesque folk architecture have been preserved. During the XVIIth century and particularly in the XVIIIth century patrician houses were built in the spirit of Late Baroque Clasicism which through the Empire style modulates in the XIXth century into Neo-styles. Houses of sea captains and shipowners follow this trend. The parish church of St George was first built in the Gothic style in the XIVth century while the net-like grooved vault of the sanctuary was built around 1470. In the XVIIIth century the church was given a Baroque quality by the addition of a number of chapels and the construction of the Baroque facade. During the 70ies of the XVth century it was painted with Late Gothic frescos and two workshops were engaged in this chore. The painting workshop from Kastav painted the vault and the upper belt of the walls while the lower

Opatija, grand Hotel "Palace"

strip with scenes of the torturing of St George is the work of the so-called "Mottled master" who also painted the scene of the Announciation in the triumphal arch.

Opatija

Opatija is the largest city on the eastern coast of Istria and the best known summer resort on the Croatian coast of the Adriatic. Its name derives from the Benedictine abbey of St Jacob. It is first mentioned during the middle of the XVth century. From the XVIth to the XVIIIth century the abbey is the possession of the Augustinians from Rijeka and from 1774 the property of the Rijeka bishopric. The present church of St Jacob was built in 1506, it was alternated in the XVIIIth century and was expanded in 1937.

As a city Opatija grew out of its role as a tourist destination which it had become by the middle of the XIXth century. When in 1843 it was connected by road to Rijeka the first architecture for tourist purposes began to be erected. In 1844 Higinio Scarpa an inhabitant of Rijeka built the villa "Angiolina" with a nicely cultivated park growing subtropical vegetation. The completion of the railroad line Wien-Trieste in 1844 with a branch line to Rijeka awoke interest in this area. In 1882 the Society of Southern Railways bought the villa "Angiolina" in Opatija and a larger complex of land. The intensive building of tourist facilities, hotels, villas, sanatoriums, baths and parks dates back to that point. The hotels "Kvarner"(1884), "Imperial" and "Opatija"(1885) and the villa "Amalia"(1890) were built during this first period. The construction of the Opatija park dates back to this period. In 1889 Opatija was proclaimed a health resort for respiratory difficulties, bronchial

Opatija, view from the sea

asthma, heart diseases, hypertonia and rheumatism. The area of Opatija was quickly urbanised and a communal infrastructure was put into place. Electrical street lamps were introduced in 1896, a water supply system a year later and trams in 1908. The buildings built during this period stretched out parallel with the waterfront with their facades turned to the sea. Cultivated greenery enriched the appearance of the city. The hotels, villas and health facilities were

The "Kvarner" hotel in Opatija was built back in 1884

Kastav

On the northeastern edge of the Istrian peninsula, high up on a hill overlooking the bay of Kvarner, 378 meters above sea level, stands the well-known town of Kastav on the old road between Rijeka and Trieste. Erected on the site of a prehistoric hill-fort Kastav, during the Middle Ages, was a significant center which included the fortified towns of Veprinac and Mošćenica. A part of its fortifications has been preserved, amongst these the fortified town gate. The municipal loggia from the XVIth century stands in front of them. A part of the fortification consists of the houses on the western and the southern walls. A cistern dating back to 1666 stands on the main square - Lokvina. The one-time captain's residence and the Gothic church of the Holy Trinity from the XVth century are also located on the square. The parish church of St Jelena is a three-naved Baroque edifice which was, like its belfry, built at the beginning of the XVIIIth century. Kastav has another interesting Baroque monument. This is the uncompleted large Jesuit church of the Holy Mary, called "Crekvina", which the Jesuits began to build in the XVIIth century in the spirit of the Roman Baroque. This is a very rare example of the style in these parts of the world. The church was never completed but ceremonies were held there up to the earthquake in 1750 when it was in large part destroyed.

In history Kastav is known for its connection to Glagolitic writing and already in the XVIth century it had a city statute written in Croatian.

Today Kastav is known because of another interesting matter. This is its folk carneval which is dominated by the picturesque masks of the so-called "zvončari" from Kastav.

The well-ordered parks in Opatija have preserved the atmosphere of the times when they were first planted at the end of the XIXth century.

Part of the hotel architecture in Opatija was done under the influence of the Wien Art Nouveau movement

built in the spirit of historical neo-styles. There are fewer examples of Secessionist architecture.

The post-WWII tourist construction followed the then contemporary trends of hotel architecture. Thusly the hotel "Ambassador" built in 1966 has a simple cubic shape while the later "Adriatic" and "Admiral" have more complex shapes.

An almost 12 kilometers long promenade alongside the sea, the famous Opatija "lungomare", stretches along the Opatija coastline from Volosko to Lovran and gives a particular charm to the city and its riviera.

The city organises a number of different cultural, entertainment and sporting events of which the majority have attained a traditional status. As a year long tourist destination Opatija is a very prominent center of congress tourism.

Contents